Churches
Aflame

Churches Aflame

Asian Americans and United Methodism

Artemio R. Guillermo

General Editor

ABINGDON PRESS
Nashville

CHURCHES AFLAME

This book is printed on recycled, acid-free paper.

Library of Congress Cataloging-in-Publication Data

Churches Aflame : Asian Americans and United Methodism / Artemio R.
  Guillermo, general editor.
      p.   cm.
    Includes bibliographical references and index.
    ISBN 0-687-08383-4 (pbk. : alk. paper)
    1. Asian American Methodists—History.   2. Methodist Church—
United States—History.   3. United Methodist Church (U.S.)
—History.   4. United States—Church history.   I. Guillermo, Artemio R.
BX8247   .A75C48   1991
287'.6'08995073—dc20   91-21909
CIP

Quotations labeled GNB are from the *Good News Bible*—Old Testament © American Bible Society 1976. Used with permission.

Quotations labeled RSV are from the Revised Standard Version of the Bible, copyright 1946, 1952, 1971 by the Division of Christian Education of the National Council of the Churches of Christ in the USA. Used with permission.

Quotations labeled KJV are from the King James, or Authorized, Version of the Bible.

95 96 97 98 99 00 01 02 03 04 — 10 9 8 7 6 5 4

C O N T E N T S

P R E F A C E

When history buffs explored abandoned mine shafts in Nevada, they uncovered a veritable village in one of them. They walked through several caverns where the walls were painted. In one room they found an altar with incense burners and benches for a small gathering. The explorers found upon further investigation that they had discovered a meeting place for Chinese who had once lived in the town above ground. While their presence in that mining town was well known, people had not realized the lengths to which the Chinese had gone to create a place where they could be themselves away from the rest of the population.

The ethnic studies that emerged in academic and community centers since the late 1960s continue to uncover the histories of people whom we have overlooked or had forced underground in order to be themselves. United Methodist leadership supported these efforts from the very beginning, which does not surprise us. In its best moments this denomination bears witness to the rich diversity in God's creative and redemptive work and celebrates the inclusive embrace in the outreach of the body of Christ. This publication provides tangible evidence of that enduring heritage. Praise be to God!

We are indebted to researchers and writers, administrators and supporters, who "surround us with so great a cloud of witnesses, so we can run with perseverance the race that is set before us" (Hebrews 12:1-2, adapted). Hallelujah!

BISHOP ROY I. SANO

ACKNOWLEDGMENTS

The General Commission on Archives and History of The United Methodist Church is pleased to be a partner in the production of this volume. It is one of the best sources available to help us remember the historic contributions of Asian American United Methodists to our church.

The General Commission is grateful to the General Conference and the General Council on Ministries for the financial support that makes the volume possible.

A number of persons have assisted in the various tasks that have resulted in this book. Members of the original Asian American consultation who designed the project included Natividad Barranda, Jonah Chang, Peter Chen, Key Ray Chong, Artemio Guillermo, Dorothy Han, James Han, Edwar Lee, Manick Samuel, Sivaji Subramanian, Lester Suzuki, and Lloyd Wake. Carolyn DeSwarte Gifford and Charles Yrigoyen, Jr., represented the staff of the General Commission.

We wish to express our appreciation to the editor and writers for the excellent work they have done in the research and writing of the essays. A special word of appreciation goes to Rebecca Marnhout who skillfully copy edited this volume.

Furthermore, we are grateful to those who carefully read the essays and offered helpful comments. The readers included Moses Lee for the Chinese chapter; I. P. Bautista, Silverio J. R. Ignacio, Roger Pangilinan, and Alex Vergara for the Filipino chapter; Shizue Yoshina for the Japanese chapter; Chan-hie Kim and Eun Chul Cho for the Korean chapter; Edwin Arthur, Victor Jacobs, and Manick Samuel for the South Asian chapter; Leon Chang and Thomas C. N. Tai for the Taiwanese chapter; and Betty Eng, Sivaji Subramanian, and Lloyd Wake for the National Federation chapter. Susan M. Eltscher of the General Commission staff has also offered invaluable help.

CHARLES YRIGOYEN, JR., *General Secretary*
General Commission on Archives and History

9

OVERVIEW

Artemio R. Guillermo

GENERAL EDITOR

United Methodists have a passion for history. We take this passion from our founder, John Wesley, who provided the model for recording events in his sensitive writings about the social, political, and economic life of eighteenth-century England. Wesley wrote with candor from his perspective as a religious leader about events, persons, and places, while infusing his message of hope and salvation to the oppressed and downtrodden.

Thus when this volume was in the offing, the consultants established one major criterion of the selection of writers: that they should have a basic knowledge of their ethnic background and a record of scholarship in the field of historical writing. Many names were presented by interested people. When the final candidates were selected, the list showed the following: three academicians, three ministers, and one young woman.

Historical writing is basically a matter of one's perspective. Thus each writer brought his or her vantage point as an active participant in the life of the church, an observer-eyewitness, or an investigative journalist. The product of their work, as this volume attests, is a colorful testimonial made vivid by their personal writing styles, selection of events, and depiction of personalities.

As the reader peruses this modest volume, one term will crop up at every turn: "Asian American." This is a demographic nomenclature that refers to people coming from the Pacific Basin, more specifically people from East Asia, namely, Chinese, Japanese, Filipinos, Malaysians, Indonesians, Indians, and the Indo-Chinese. The word originally used, "Oriental," was too restrictive and pejorative, so it was dropped in favor of "Asian American," a term felt by the various ethnic caucuses contributing to this book to be more inclusive and attractive.

While this volume is the first of its type to be put out by the General Commission on Archives and History, it has no pretensions about being definitive, exhaustive, and scholarly. Each writer tried his or her best to encompass the length and breadth of recorded history, as long as it would fit "within 45 typewritten pages, double spaced," which was the order given for reasons of space limitations. However, since most of our Asian American churches have been established fairly recently, much will remain for the next batch of historians to write about in the necessary sequel to this book, to cover new congregations presently being organized by the ethnic churches.

During the planning stage of this volume, the consultants laid down a simple objective for this work: to provide a popular and comprehensive one-volume history of the various Asian American United Methodist churches in the United States to be used as resource material for the Ethnic Minority Local Church Missional Emphasis. This volume, which required more than three years of work by the writers, from outline to several drafts, is an attempt to piece together the significant events and episodes that led to the formation of the ethnic churches and to present in a handy reference the kaleidoscopic witness of Asian American churches in the United Methodist tradition.

If there is one word that would best describe the development of our Asian American United Methodist churches, it would be "struggle." In my view this word summarizes the birthing, dramatic lives, and triumph against all odds of these fledgling churches in an often hostile environment. Like their ancient brethren, the Israelites, Asian Americans wandered in this vast land of opportunity on an uncertain faith journey. The analogy is not far-fetched, for Asian Americans had to fight their way through, not with swords but with voices, often discordant until their pleas for identity were heard. For it is this innate desire for identity in the midst of diversity in the household of faith that propelled their struggle to get to the Promised Land.

The struggle was not so much against physical forces that could be vanquished as against the subtle and malignant forces of racism, discrimination, and bigotry. To combat these forces required indomitable faith in God and in the justness of their cause. And like the Israelites, the Asian Americans persevered in their struggle, for the Lord waited on them as they mounted with wings as eagles. The God of Abraham and Jacob did not fail them.

None of these Asian American churches could have survived without guardian angels in the persons of Anglos (whites) who staked their lives and fortunes on ethnic leaders who continuously voiced their wishes before Annual Conferences and the higher councils of the church. One of these Anglos, for example, was Dr. Otis Gibson, whose name looms large in the formation of Japanese and Chinese Methodist churches on the West Coast. A former missionary in Fukien, China, he was appointed together with his wife to develop the ministry among the Chinese in San Francisco. They spent the better part of their lifetimes championing the cause of the Chinese, even appearing in court in defense of Chinese who has been wrongly haled there.

His effigy was burned by anti-Chinese mobs. Gibson rightly earned the title of Founder of the Chinese Methodist Mission. Eventually he went on to found the Japanese Methodist Mission on the West Coast, which proliferated into Japanese Methodist congregations in California, Washington, and Colorado.

The struggle would not be complete without mentioning the struggle within the ranks of Asian American leaders. This inside struggle was even more debilitating. Although the writers may have glossed over this episode in their historical accounts, there is no gainsaying that some ethnic congregations did go through this baptism of fire. This struggle was among persons who were after the power and influence as well as the status and prestige bestowed on those in leadership positions. One ethnic church (which will not be identified in this overview) had to go through a most difficult birthing process because of power struggles among its leaders, which as a consequence splintered the congregation. When the smoke of the battle cleared, only a remnant of the original membership was left, but this remnant continued on their faith journey with greater strength and renewed zeal. Today this church is leading an evangelistic program that is discipling more members to its fold. God is faithful to those who persevere.

The growth of Asian American United Methodist churches chronicled in this volume is an effect of changes of the immigration laws of the United States. Asian Americans came into this country in two waves. With the first wave came the laborers, manual workers recruited to work the cane and pineapple fields of Hawaii and the railroads of the West Coast. Most of them were illiterate. These early comers were mostly Chinese and Japanese. The second wave occurred after a major change in immigration law occurring in 1965, which allowed various categories of immigrants to enter the United States; in this wave came Filipinos, Koreans, and Indians. These new immigrants were mostly professionals and educated persons, as in the case of Filipino doctors, nurses, engineers, professors, and teachers. Many of these Asian immigrants settled in cities and urban areas where their skills and arts were in demand and wisely put to use.

These new citizens became the group sought for ministry by the various Asian ethnic caucuses. This ministry became more visible when the national caucuses brought to the attention of the general church the urgency of opening new ministries to reach this new wave of immigrants. The church responded by adopting the missional priority of Local Minority Local Church, which ran for two quadrennia (1980 to 1988).

The Koreans were the first to take off in new church development, and their growth over the years has been phenomenal. In every major city and metroplex there are Korean United Methodist churches ministering to their people. They are indeed the fastest growing ethnic church within our denomination. Following the Koreans are the Filipinos and the Indo-Chinese.

Indeed, the membership of The United Methodist Church has been enriched by the presence of Asian American congregations. This communion of believers brought with them their own particularity and the rich patina of their cultures, which overlies their programs and worship services. With the resources provided by the church, the increase in membership of Asian American United Methodist congregations has helped stem the tide of the denomination's membership loss over the past decade.

The growth of ethnic congregations confirms the truth that churches grow not by the power of individuals but rather by the power of the Holy Spirit working in the hearts and souls of devout men and women. This power continues to move within the hearts of Asian American churches and continues to prevail among their leaders, giving them new vision of the future that can be.

C O N T R I B U T O R S

Helen Kuang Chang, author of the history of Formosan United Methodist churches, was born in Chang Hwa, Taiwan, in 1962 and emigrated to the United States when she was five years old. Her father is Jonah Chang. She studied mass communications at the University of California, Berkeley, receiving her B.A. with high honors in 1980. Upon graduation, she worked as a radio traffic reporter and radio station account representative before becoming interpretation assistant for the General Board of Church and Society in Washington, D.C. Currently, she works as assistant manager in public relations with the San Francisco Convention Bureau.

Jonah Jui-Hsiung Chang, author of the history of the National Federation of Asian American United Methodists, is a native of Taiwan. He obtained his theological training in a Presbyterian seminary in Taiwan. He served as a Presbyterian pastor before emigrating to the United States in 1962. In 1967 he joined The United Methodist Church and served Japanese-American churches in California. He became executive director of the Western Jurisdiction Asian American Ministries in 1973. Two years later, he became the founding executive director of the National Federation of Asian American United Methodists, in which position he served for ten years. In 1988 he was appointed district superintendent of the Bay View District of the California-Nevada Conference.

Key Ray Chong, principal author of the history of Korean United Methodist churches, is an associate professor of history at Texas Tech University in Lubbock. He obtained his B.A. from Aoyama Gakuin University, Tokyo, Japan; his M.A. from the University of Washington, and his Ph.D. from Claremont Graduate School. He has taught at the University of Maine,

Orono, and at Drury College. He has published articles in a number of history journals in both the United States and South Korea. In past years he has served as vice president of the National Association of Korean American United Methodists. During the summer of 1987 he worked as chief researcher of the oral history project of the Asian American United Methodists, sponsored by the General Commission on Archives and History.

Myong Gul Son works as an assistant general secretary, parish ministries unit, in the General Board of Global Ministries, New York.

Artemio R. Guillermo, author of the history of Filipino American United Methodist churches, holds an M.A. (journalism) and Ph.D. (communication) from Syracuse University, where he studied as a Fulbright and Crusade scholar. He worked as a religious journalist in the Philippines, reporting for the Religious News Service (New York) and the National Council of Christian Churches. Later he was hired by Procter & Gamble Philippines as a brand manager for its consumer products. Then he transferred to the United States Educational Foundation in the Philippines and became their program officer. In the United States, he taught journalism and public relations at Bowling Green State University, Arkansas State University, and the University of Northern Iowa. He was elected lay delegate to the 1984 General Conference in Baltimore. Currently, he serves as chairperson of the Iowa Conference Committee on Planning and Research and as national president of the National Filipino American United Methodists in the United States.

Lester E. Suzuki, author of the history of Japanese United Methodist churches, is a retired United Methodist minister with a service record of forty-two years. Ordained a minister in 1938 and an elder in 1940, he ministered to churches in California, Iowa, and Washington. He obtained his B.A. from San Jose State University, his B.D. and M.A. from Drew University, and his D.Min. from San Francisco Theological Seminary. During World War II he was interned in the Amache Relocation Center as one of the thousands of Japanese Americans put in concentration camps. Out of this experience he wrote a book, *Ministry in the Assembly and Relocation Centers of World War II,* published in 1979.

Wilbur Wong Yan Choy, author of the history of Chinese American United Methodist churches, is a retired bishop of The United Methodist Church; he served in the Seattle and San Francisco episcopal areas. He holds a B.D. from the College of the Pacific, an M.Div. from the Pacific School of Religion, and honorary doctorates from the Pacific School of Religion and the University of Puget Sound. Ordained an elder in 1946, he served churches in California and was appointed district superintendent of Bay View District. He was elected to the episcopacy in 1972. During his episcopal term he served as president of the Council of Bishops and as a trustee of his alma maters, Pacific School of Religion, University of Puget Sound, the School of Theology at Claremont, and the University of the Pacific. He lives in retirement in Spokane, Washington, with his wife, Nancy Yamasaki, an ordained United Methodist minister.

Man Singh Das, author of the history of South Asian United Methodist Churches, is a professor of sociology at Northern Illinois University at DeKalb and an ordained United Methodist minister in the Northern Illinois Conference. He obtained his B.S., B.D., and M.Th. degrees from Indian universities and his Th.M (comparative religions), M.A. (education), M.A. (sociology), and Ph.D. (sociology) from American universities. He serves as general secretary of the International Association of Family Sociology and is editor and founder of two international journals. He also serves as an associate editor of nine sociological journals. He has published numerous scientific articles and ten books. His major works are *Brain Drain Controversy, The Family in Asia, The Family in Latin America,* and *Sociocultural Change Since 1950.*

C H A P T E R   1

SOJOURNERS IN THE LAND OF THE FREE:

History of Southern Asian United Methodist Churches

Man Singh Das

The subcontinent of South Asia covers a vast region incorporating India, Pakistan, Bangladesh, Nepal, Thailand, Indonesia, Malaysia, Sri Lanka, Burma, Singapore, and others, all nations having a common ancestral and cultural heritage. The goal of this chapter is not to write about the fellowship groups or churches formed by immigrants from any one of these nations but to write about all South Asian churches in general. Originally the scope of this chapter was limited to Southern Asian United Methodist churches; however, the analysis was expanded to cover all other denominations. The main purpose in studying all the denominations was to (1) get a clear picture of Southern Asians and (2) gather data useful for developing United Methodist churches and fellowship groups among them, especially where the groups or the leaders were not committed to a particular denomination.

LEGISLATIVE BACKGROUND OF SOUTHERN ASIAN IMMIGRATION

Immigration policy in the United States has a complex history. There have essentially been four broad phases of American immigration experience.

Phase I: 1776 to 1875

The earliest immigration from India supposedly took place during the years 1776 to 1875, a time referred to as "the period of free immigration."

According to a colonial diary entry written by the Reverend William Bentley of Salem, Massachusetts, on December 29, 1790, the first arrival from India in the United States was probably from Madras in South India.[1] During this period of free immigration, only a small number of people, mostly Parsis from Bombay, came to the United States (see Table 1.1). Parsis, followers of Zoroastrianism, are a small religious and ethnic minority, but they constitute an elite and relatively wealthy business community in India.

TABLE 1.1 ASIAN INDIAN IMMIGRANTS TO THE
UNITED STATES, 1820 to 1984

Decade–Year	Number of Immigrants	Total for all Years
1820	1	
1821–1830	8	
1831–1840	39	
1841–1850	36	
1851–1860	43	
1861–1870	69	
1871–1880	163	
1881–1890	269	
1891–1900	68	
1901–1910	4,713	
1911–1920	2,082	
1921–1930	1,886	
1931–1940	496	
1941–1950	1,761	
1951–1960	1,973	
1961–1970	27,189	
1971–1980	164,134	
1981	21,522	
1982	21,738	
1983	25,451	
1984	23,617	297,258

Source: U.S. Department of Justice Immigration and Naturalization Service, *Statistical Yearbook of the Immigration and Naturalization Service* (Washington, D.C.: U.S. Government Printing Office, 1984).

Phase II: 1875 to 1921

The policy of free immigration gradually gave way to qualitative restrictions. In 1882 the Chinese Exclusion Act was passed. In 1917 this act was extended to all Asians. Also excluded in the 1880s, under pressure from organized labor, were contract laborers.

Phase III: 1921 to 1964

A few years later, in 1921 and 1924, Congress enacted two immigration acts popularly known as the National Origins Quotas acts. These quota laws excluded Asian Indians because of their previous barring in 1917.

It was not until the passage of the Immigration Act of 1946 that Asian Indians were officially included in the immigration acts. This act officially authorized the admission of Asian Indians into the United States and made them racially eligible for naturalization and other purposes.[2]

Phase IV: 1964 to Present

Subsequent acts of 1952 and 1965 further opened ways for immigration from Asia into this country. Asians took advantage of the professional preference categories to move to the United States or to adjust from student or business visas to permanent resident status. After five years of permanent residence they could become citizens and then were eligible to bring in relatives without numerical restrictions under the family reunification provisions of the preference system. Eventually these relatives could in the same way enlarge their family groups in the United States. As a result of this "chain immigration" process, the number of Asian Indian immigrants sharply increased during the two decades, 1961–1970 and 1971–1980 (see Table 1.1).

Demographic and Social Characteristics of South Asian Immigrants

The Immigration Act of 1965, which abolished the national origins quota system and established a system of preference categories, has made it possible for Asians and particularly Asian Indians to immigrate in large numbers to the United States every year. As a result, today's immigration is changing the ethnic composition of the United States' population.

Education and Employment of Asian Indians

We find that both men and women are entering this country in equal numbers, and that the largest age group of people comprises those 20 to 29 years old. It is interesting to note that a significant number of retired people are also coming here as immigrants, which may have serious ramifications for the South Asian church.

In comparison with other Asian immigrants, Asian Indians appear to have the highest level of education. A large percentage of Asian Indians are professionals, and the majority of them are gainfully employed. One should not be surprised to note that because of the high educational attainment and professional status of Asian Indians, the median income for both men and women with full-time jobs is also higher than that for other Asian immigrants in this country.

Areas of Heavy Concentration of Asian Indians in the United States

According to the 1980 United States census report, there were 361,544 Asian Indians in the United States (see Table 1.2). Asian Indians constituted about two tenths of 1 percent of the total American population of 226.5 million. Since the 1980 census, another 92,328 people from India have immigrated to this country, between 1981 and 1984 (see Table 1.1). This would mean that the total number of Asian Indians in 1984 was approximately 453,872.

TABLE 1.2 REGIONAL DISTRIBUTION OF ASIAN INDIANS IN THE UNITED STATES

Region	Total	Percent	Total Estimate of Asian Indian Christians*
Northeast	120,761	33	3,623
North Central	85,119	24	2,554
South	83,586	23	2,507
West	72,078	20	2,162
Total	361,544	100	10,845

Source: The U.S. Bureau of the Census, *The 1980 Census Report*.

Note: *Northeast* includes Maine, New Hampshire, Vermont, Massachusetts, Rhode Island, Connecticut, New York, New Jersey, and Pennsylvania. *North Central* includes Ohio, Indiana, Illinois, Michigan, Wisconsin, Minnesota, Iowa, Missouri, North Dakota, South Dakota, Nebraska, and Kansas. *South* consists of Delaware, Maryland, District of Columbia, Virginia, West Virginia, North and South Carolinas, Georgia, Florida, Kentucky, Tennessee, Alabama, Arkansas, Louisiana, Oklahoma, and Texas. *West* includes Montana, Idaho, Wyoming, Colorado, New Mexico, Arizona, Utah, Nevada, Washington, Oregon, California, Alaska, and Hawaii.

* Estimate based on 1983 United Nations estimate that 3 percent of the total population of India is Christian. Other demographic variables controlled for in the calculation.

The 1980 census report indicates that most Asian Indians are concentrated in five states: New York, California, Illinois, New Jersey, and Texas (see Table 1.3).

TABLE 1.3 CONCENTRATION OF ASIAN INDIANS
IN THE VARIOUS STATES

State	*Total*	*Percent*	*Total Estimate of Asian Indian Christians**
States with 20,000 and More Asian Indian Population			
New York	60,511	17	1,815
California	57,989	16	1,740
Illinois	35,711	10	1,071
New Jersey	29,507	8	885
Texas	22,226	6	667
States with 13,000 to 15,000 Asian Indians			
Pennsylvania	15,212	5	456
Michigan	14,680	4	440
Maryland	13,705	3.7	411
Ohio	13,105	3.6	393
States with 8,000 to 10,000 Asian Indians			
Florida	9,138	2.5	274
Virginia	8,483	2.4	254
Massachusetts	8,387	2.3	252
States with 4,000 to 5,000 Asian Indians			
Connecticut	4,995	1.4	150
North Carolina	4,718	1.3	142
Georgia	4,347	1.2	130
Indiana	4,290	1.2	129
Missouri	4,099	1.1	123
Washington	4,002	1.1	120
States with Least Asian Indian Concentration			
North Dakota	294	0.08	9
Alaska	241	0.06	7
South Dakota	182	0.05	5
Wyoming	176	0.04	5
Montana	162	0.04	4

Source: U.S. Bureau of the Census, *The 1980 Census Report* (Washington, D.C.: U.S. Government Printing Office, 1980).

Note: In 1980 there were 361,544 Asian Indians, and they constituted about two-tenths of 1 percent of the total 26.5 million.

* Estimate based on 1983 United Nations estimate that 3% of the total population of India is Christian. Other demographic variables controlled for in the calculation.

Since we are dealing here with South Asian churches, our primary attention should be focused on South Asian Christian communities. The recent report published by the General Board of Global Ministries about the distribution of racial and ethnic minorities in The United Methodist Church has lumped all Asians into a single category.[3] Therefore, it is difficult to give estimates of the number of Asian Indian Christians in the United States.

CONTRIBUTING FACTORS IN THE EMERGENCE OF A VIABLE SOUTHERN ASIAN CHURCH

Factors in the emergence of a viable South Asian church are as follows.

Religious Experience of South Asians

Most South Asian Christians who have come to this country are from a first- or second-generation Christian family. In most cases they or their families have been converted by American or European missionaries. Conversion in South Asia has a deep religious and emotional significance. In many cases these families have had to make personal sacrifices in order to accept Christ. In some cases they have been ostracized by their extended families and their community because they have embraced a new, foreign religion. It was important for these Christians, then, to have a church home to help them overcome some of the losses they had experienced.

Brain Drain of South Asian Church

In the past, South Asian church leaders and particularly Indian bishops have complained that the Indian church has been robbed of its talent by emigration to the United States. According to various studies of the "brain drain" experienced by many less-developed nations, it has been found that most South Asians, including ministers, who come to the United States for higher studies do not return to their home countries upon completion of their studies.[4]

Without getting into a debate on the significance of this brain drain, one thing seems clear: The United States has benefited tremendously from the flow of these professionals into this country. If it is a brain drain to the church in India, it may be argued that it is a "brain gain" to the church in the United States.

At present there are about twenty Asian Indian ministers in this country, and fifteen of them belong to The United Methodist Church. Most of them graduated from the Leonard Theological College (a Methodist institution), a seminary frequently referred to as the Indian Harvard Divinity School.

Many of them came to this country at the end of the 1950s and the beginning of the 1960s, a period during which the civil rights movement was very active. It will be difficult to list each and every thing they did for the development of South Asian churches in this country. It can be easily said that many of the Leonard graduates are behind the establishing of new fellowship groups, churches, regional and national caucuses, and Christian organizations in this country.

During the early 1960s, when there was massive civil and racial unrest in this country, South Asian ministers were in great demand because of their culture, training, and language background. The Reverend Victor Jacobs (who is now with the Board of Discipleship); Bishop Stanley Downes, a Methodist bishop in India who later returned to India; the author of this chapter (who was the first Asian Indian to be ordained by the Northern Illinois Conference), and the Reverend Edwin J. Arthur (in New York) were the first Asian Indian ministers to serve in integrated United Methodist churches in the Chicago area and New York.

Home Country Church Link

Methodist bishops in India have strongly urged people to start Asian Indian churches in this country. They felt that Asian Indian churches would make it possible for them to maintain strong ties with the church in India, and also that the church in India could count on their support for special projects.

Demographic Factors

The biggest change in South Asian immigrant population took place after the passage of the Immigration Act of 1965. From 1951 to 1960 there were about 1,973 Asian Indian immigrants in the nation; that number rose sharply to 27,189 in the years from 1961 to 1970. The biggest jump in the number of Asian Indian immigrants took place from 1971 to 1980, when some 164,134 people entered this country. The favorable demographic factors in the late 1960s and early 1970s made it possible for many South Asian leaders to start fellowship groups and churches, because these immigrants had many social needs, and their cultural diversity increased. One might be tempted to suggest that before someone can be a leader, there must be people ready to be led. The more differences you see in a population, the more groups are likely to be organized within it.

Social Situations Favoring the Emergence of South Asian Churches

During the times of racial turmoil and the civil rights movement in the 1960s, black Methodist churches organized a black caucus in the church, and in 1965 they demanded funds to be used exclusively for black churches and to be administered by the black caucus. This writer attended the special session of the Northern Illinois Conference called for discussion of black issues of the time. At this meeting there was a heated debate, at the end of which the dominant Methodist church agreed to meet the just demands of black Methodist churches.

This was the beginning of an emphasis on the inclusive nature of the church. The following year Spanish church leaders presented their demands, and afterward Asians came forward with their requests. The attitude of the white Methodist church changed from exclusiveness to inclusiveness, and as a result the dominant white church was ready to help and encourage the development of new ministries for various ethnic churches in this country. South Asian Methodists, along with other racial and ethnic groups, were able to take full advantage of this change in attitude, and as a result they were able to organize fellowship groups and churches to meet the sociocultural needs of their people.

CULTURAL DIVERSITY

India is a culturally diversified society, in that there are (1) major regional differences between north and south; (2) subregional differences—there are twenty-two states and nine territories; (3) linguistic differences—there are fourteen major languages; (4) religious differences—Hindus (83%), Moslems (11%), Christians (3%), Sikhs (2%), and Buddhists and others (1%) coexist there; and (5), among Christians, denominational differences. Each social group in India has a distinct culture, which is also noticeable in Asian Indian churches in this country.

Most of the Asian Indian churches and fellowship groups are developed along regional and linguistic lines. The following lists some examples:

1. Gujarati Prayer Fellowship (organized by Ramesh Das in 1977)
2. Gujarati Fellowship (organized by John Rathod in 1978)
3. Gujarati Fellowship (organized by Edmond Christian of Chicago in 1982)
4. Hindi Fellowship (organized by Isaac Cornelius of Skokie, Illinois, in 1976)
5. India Christian Telugu Church, now called India Mission United Methodist Church (organized by a group of Telugu Christians led by Samuel Vallabadas in 1975)
6. India-Pakistan Church of Chicago (organized by the Reverend Ernest C. Singh of Chicago in 1983)
7. South Asian Community Church (organized by the author in 1987)

Persons from South India in this country may be divided into three dominant linguistic groups Telugu: Tamil, and Malayalam. Telugu fellowship groups and churches tend to be larger in size and more interdenominational in make-up.

STAGES OF DEVELOPMENT OF SOUTHERN ASIAN CHURCHES

The formative stages of early South Asian church development are described in the diagram below:

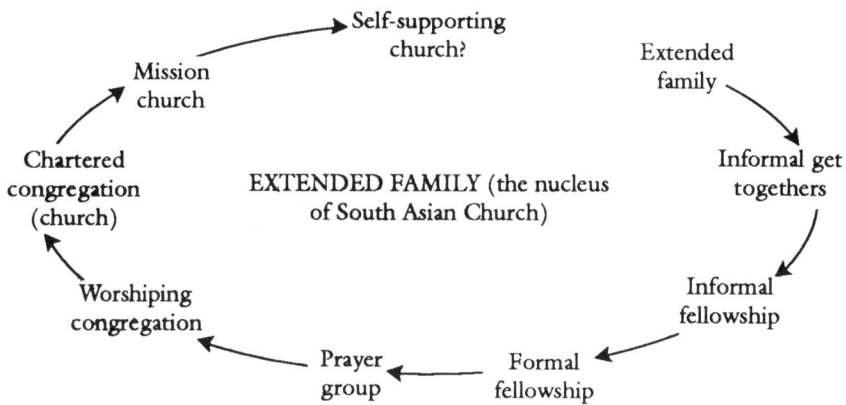

Self-supporting
church?
Extended
family

Mission
church

Informal get
togethers

Chartered
congregation
(church)

EXTENDED FAMILY (the nucleus
of South Asian Church)

Worshiping
congregation

Informal
fellowship

Prayer
group

Formal
fellowship

A comparative analysis along with church affiliation of both the organizers and members of South Asian churches may be useful for ascertaining how the development of South Asian United Methodist churches is going to occur. A detailed list of all the South Asian churches, worshiping congregations, and fellowships in The United Methodist Church, organized by date of founding, is given in appendix 1-A. Since the list is self-explanatory, the below provides highlights of the development of these South Asian United Methodist churches.

The First Indian Fellowship

The first Indian Fellowship was organized by Victor Jacobs, Stanley Downes, and the author in the Chicago area in 1964. This group had about thirty to thirty-five members (all the Asian Indian Christians in Chicago at that time). They used to meet regularly once a month in homes and churches for potlucks, fellowship, prayer, and study. In 1966 the fellowship group split into two due to ideological, theological, philosophical, and organizational differences. One group (about fifteen people) went with the Reverend Bharat

Bhooshan (formerly a Methodist but now with the United Church of Christ in Highland, Illinois). The other stayed with Jacobs, Downes, and Das. The Indian Fellowship led by Bhooshan finally disbanded in 1968 when all the organizers moved to other states.

The First Asian Indian Church in the United States

In 1969 a small group of people in Chicago from different parts of India started meeting in homes for prayer and fellowship at the request of Brother Bhakt Singh of India. Brother Bhakt Singh is a famous evangelist and a Hindu convert. The group's first meeting was in the home of Samuel Vallabadas, a Methodist from South India who eventually became a lay pastor of First India Mission United Methodist Church, in 1983. The group continued to meet between 1969 and 1973, and the membership grew to about three hundred persons. The first Asian Indian church, called India Christian Fellowship Church, was finally chartered in 1973. George Shriner and Dean Overhoulser, the pastors of the United Church of the Medical Center (United Church belongs to both the United Methodist and Presbyterian churches), gave all the support and encouragement in getting this historical church chartered.

The first pastor of this nondenominational church was the Reverend M. J. Thomas. The present pastor is the Reverend Devasahayam Godwin. The associate pastor is a Methodist. The church has a well-organized ministry and is self-supporting. In 1975 the church split into several groups due to linguistic differences.

The First India Mission United Methodist Church in the United States

One of the splinter groups from the India Christian Fellowship Church was led by Samuel Vallabadas in 1975. Most of the members were Telugu-speaking Methodists. They organized India Christian Telugu Church, whose name was later changed to India Mission United Methodist Church. The present pastor of the church is Vallabadas. Most of the members of this church are professionals, and the church is self-supporting. The church has not been chartered yet.

The First India-Pakistan Chartered United Methodist Church in the United States

Hope United Methodist Church of Philadelphia was organized in 1985 by a group of people including Salim Khan, Salim Barkat, Anwar Alam, the Reverend John V. Bhajjan, and the Reverend Samuel Ramnit, and it was fully chartered on April 19, 1987. The church has 100 percent Indo-Pak membership and has a South Asian pastor, the Reverend John V. Bhajjan.

28

The First South Asian Community Church

South Asian Community Church of Chicago was organized on Thanksgiving Day, 1987, by the author, with the encouragement and cooperation of Fourth Street United Methodist Church of Aurora, Illinois.

The First Hindi Fellowship

The first Hindi fellowship was organized in 1976 by Isaac Cornelius, formerly a Reformed Presbyterian minister who later joined The United Methodist Church. The group moved to Emmanuel Methodist Church in Evanston, Illinois, in 1978, where it has become an integral part of the church. Pastor Cornelius died in 1985. The present pastor of this group is Timothy Rathod, a member of The United Methodist Church.

The First Gujarati Fellowship

The first Gujarati fellowship was organized by Ramesh Das, in 1977 in Temple City, California. This fellowship group has developed into the La Canada United Methodist Church (the mother church) with two other daughter churches in Orange County and San Fernando Valley. All three groups hold their fellowships separately; however, once a month they all meet together. Their apportionments go toward the support of various projects in Gujarat.

The First Asian Indian Pastor to Serve
Mixed Anglo-American and Asian Indian Congregations

John Rathod organized the Gujarati Fellowship in 1978. Both the Hindi and the Gujarati fellowships became an integral part of the Emmanuel Methodist Church in Evanston, Illinois, in 1984, when he was appointed as the pastor of that church. The church has about 171 members, and three separate worship services are concluded in Gujarati, Hindi (Hindi pastor, the Reverend Timothy Rathod), and English. The church has a combined worship service of *all* three groups on the first Sunday of every month. The average attendance is about 35 people at every separate ethnic worship service. The church has started a radio ministry; the radio program is aired every Sunday for half an hour in Gujarati and Hindi.

PROGNOSIS OF SOUTH ASIAN CHURCHES

The prognosis of South Asian churches appears to be excellent. However, the ultimate outcome will depend upon the attitude of various culturally diversified groups within the South Asian community and the level of cooperation between the South Asian community and the Anglo-American (white-dominant) church.

Demographers specializing in migration diagnose three groups of South Asians who have come to this country over a period of time: the first generation (new and old, born in India or elsewhere), the second generation (children born in this country), and nonimmigrants here for a specified purpose who are expected to return home upon realization of their goal. In some instances the cultural diversity of South Asian immigrants; their search for a new quadripartite identity based on nation, region, and local, and linguistic factors); factionalism based on the extended family and interpersonal rivalries have created conflicts within the South Asian community. These conflicts had an inhibiting effect in the early stages of the development of a variable South Asian church. In addition, the original settlement of these immigrants was strictly region and folk oriented. Economic and material adjustment to their new country was more important for first-generation South Asian immigrants than cultural, social, and religious adjustment, which also had a dysfunctional effect on the early South Asian church. When viewed from an Anglo-American perspective, they were perceived as the manifestation of negative character traits; as a result the United Methodist hierarchy (media, boards, and agencies) was either indifferent to the just needs of the South Asian community or gave lukewarm support for the development of their churches.

As the young South Asian community becomes a more mature group, the level of conflict within and among the community's various groups is likely to diminish and have less negative effect on the development of a viable South Asian church. There are so many positives about the South Asian community, such as its extended family system; deep religious convictions; number of qualified clergy available; home country church link; related social and demographic factors; cultural diversity; strong national organization of its clergy, laity, churches, and fellowship groups; and the positive attitude of the United Methodist hierarchy (including boards and agencies) and the Anglo-American church in general. All of these are going to have a eufunctional effect in the development of South Asian churches.

IMPLICATIONS FOR THE DEVELOPMENT OF A VIABLE SOUTH ASIAN UNITED METHODIST CHURCH

Originally, my purpose was to write the history of South Asian churches in this country; however, I felt that such an undertaking was far too difficult. Instead, I would like to underline certain implications of our analysis of the South Asian community.

1. In 1984, according to the estimates computed by the author, there were approximately 13,616 Asian Indian Christians in this country, and the majority of them were Methodists. The United Methodist hierarchy (including the Anglo-American church, boards, and agencies) has either been indifferent or given lukewarm support to these immigrants.

2. According to vital statistics there are approximately 453,872 Asian Indians in this country. No programs have been developed by either the South Asian church or the Anglo-American church to meet their social and spiritual needs.

3. The number of South Asian nonimmigrants admitted to this country has been increasing every year. For instance, in 1984 there were 103,783 Asian Indians; 32,213 Pakistanis; 44,019 Malaysians, and 31,028 from Singapore. These nonimmigrants have been treated as orphans by both the South Asian church and the Anglo-American church.

4. New York, California, Illinois, New Jersey, and Texas have huge concentrations of Asian Indian immigrants. The concept of circuit riders or "the ministry of presence" was recommended by the South Asian Caucus as a model of ministry to these groups (see Table 1.4).

5. All Asians are lumped together in a single category by the Office of Research of the General Board of Global Ministries. Since South Asians have a diversified culture, it may be advisable to have a separate category for each country.

TABLE 1.4 COMPARISON OF ASIAN INDIAN POPULATION WITH
OTHER ASIAN AND PACIFIC AMERICANS
IN THE UNITED STATES

States	Total	Asian Indian	Rank*
All United States**	3,500,638	361,544	4
New York	310,531	60,511	2
California	1,253,987	57,989	6
Illinois	159,551	35,711	2
New Jersey	103,842	29,507	1
Texas	120,306	22,226	3

Source: The Bureau of the Census, *The 1980 Census Report* (Washington, D.C.: U.S. Government Printing Office, 1980).

* The rank of other preceding Asian and Pacific populations, in order of their respective numerical sizes: *all United States*—Chinese (1), Filipino (2), and Japanese (3); *New York*—Chinese (1); *California*—Filipino (1), Chinese (2), Japanese (3), Korean (4), Vietnamese (5); *Illinois*—Filipino (1); *Texas*—Vietnamese (1), Chinese (2).

** According to the 1980 census figures, these are 6,756,986 *Others.*

6. The United Methodist hierarchy (including various boards and agencies that deal with the problem of ethnic minorities) may want to retain a South Asian as a consultant or a resource person who has expertise and who understands the complexities and dynamics of the South Asian community. The consultant could be very helpful in the development of new congregations and in evangelism for all South Asians.

7. About 97 percent of Asian Indian immigrants are non-Christians; the majority of these are Hindus (83 percent) and Moslems (11 percent). Since the process of Americanization and Christianization of these immigrants has already started on its own, a comprehensive program should be developed to evangelize and provide Christian care to these people.

8. Our study suggests that the SANCUM is the only national organization of clergy, laity, churches, and fellowship groups that has denominational support. Since its founding in 1980, the SANCUM has played vital roles in holding clergy consultations (in 1982, Chicago and Pasadena, California, and in 1985 in Nashville), in publishing *South Asian American News*, and in compiling two national directories of South Asian Christians and youth. Now attempts are being made to bring all South Asian Christians together. Various United Methodist boards and agencies may want to strengthen the hands of the SANCUM so that it may be able to develop various outreach ministries.

9. Chicago has emerged as the mecca of South Asian Christians. The first Indian Christian Fellowship Church was organized there in 1969. The church is still not affiliated with any denomination. The United Methodist Church may want to take initiatives to attracting these believers to our fellowship due to their membership composition, strategic location, and the denominational affiliation of their pastors (the associate pastor is a United Methodist).

10. The first India Mission United Methodist Church was founded in 1975; efforts should be made to have this church chartered.

11. West Devon in Chicago has been referred to as "Little India." Because of the proximity of Granville United Methodist Church and the presence and enthusiasm of a Gujarati fellowship, encouragement should be given to this church to develop a ministry for non-Christians.

12. A South Asian ministry exists in Glen Ellyn, Illinois. The organizing pastor is a Methodist, and the majority of people involved are Methodists. The United Methodist Church should start consultations with these people to see if a church could be chartered.

13. Emmanuel United Methodist Church in Evanston, Illinois, which has mixed Anglo-American and Asian Indian congregations and an Asian Indian pastor, has become a symbolic Asian Indian church and should be given necessary support in developing new ministries for unchurched people.

CONCLUSIONS

Senator Edward M. Kennedy in 1966 said before the U.S. Senate, "A measure of greatness for any nation is its ability to recognize past errors in judgment and its willingness to reform its public policy." We would like to paraphrase this and suggest that measure of greatness for any church is its ability to recognize past errors in judgment and its willingness to reform its racial and ethnic minority policy.

No organized effort has been made by any church denomination in this country to provide Christian care to thousands of non-Christian immigrants. The United Methodist Church may well argue that its ministries and programs are not designed to solve the social and religious problems of all immigrants.

On the one hand, traditionalists are attempting to raise their South Asian American-born children like those reared in South Asia. They are insisting upon preserving their ethnic institutions, particularly those pertaining to religion, language, endogamous marriage, and the extended family. On the other hand, "environmentalists" (also known as assimilationists) believe that their children should be primarily raised as Americans but want them to retain their membership in a South Asian church, keep their South Asian names, and be able to communicate in a South Asian language. These South Asians feel that the assimilation process cannot be curtailed but only temporarily delayed.

As long as there is agreement between traditionalists, environmentalists, and The United Methodist Church (Anglo-American church) in general about the eufunctional effect of an ethnic church, the South Asian church will continue to grow in this country. Generally South Asians are church-oriented people, and they need a church that is community oriented. This means that the survival of one depends on the survival of the other.

The long-dominant Anglo-American church has become more receptive to the idea of cultural pluralism. What will happen when no ethnic majority exists, as is already the case in Hawaii and will be in California and Texas soon after the turn of the century? Will "assimilation into" become "assimilation among," and how will the dominant Anglo-American church react? It is time to ask, What kind of church do we want in the twenty-first century? Peter Schuck, Yale University professor, puts the question this way: "What are we? What do we wish to become? And most fundamentally, which individuals constitute the 'we' who shall decide these questions?"[5]

NOTES

1. William Bentley, *The Diary of William Bentley* (Salem, Mass.: The Essex Institute, 1962), vol. 1, p. 228.
2. *United States Statutes at Large* (Washington, D.C.: U.S. Government Printing Office, 1946), vol. 1, p. 416.

3. Office of Research, National Program Division, *Distribution of Racial-Ethnic Minorities in the United Methodist Church* (New York: General Board of Global Ministries, 1985).

4. Man Singh Das, "Brain Drain Controversy and Utilization of Returning Indian Scholars Trained Abroad," *Population Review* 21 (Jan.-Dec., 1977): 28-36.

5. Peter H. Schuck, "Immigration Law and the Problem of Community," in Nathan Glazer, *Clamor at the Gates* (San Francisco: Institute for Contemporary Studies, 1985), pp. 285-286.

C H A P T E R 2

BIRTHING OF A CHURCH:

History of Formosan United Methodist Churches

Helen Kuang Chang

There is an old Taiwanese saying that in every Formosan runs the blood of the Pi^n-Po people (a Chinese designation for the civilized native people of Taiwan). It is also said that if someone were to scratch Taiwan's doctors, teachers, and other well-educated professionals, he or she would find evidence of Pi^n-Po heritage, for at one time, the saying goes, the Pi^n-Po people civilized the Chinese invaders who "conquered" Taiwan. So from the proud, intelligent native people of Taiwan stems the Formosan identity.

Understanding this Formosan identity and the historical circumstances leading to its formation is critical to understanding the Taiwanese United Methodist church in the United States.

SOCIOCULTURAL BACKGROUND

Portuguese sailors in the late 1500s landed on the shores of the biggest of the Pescadore Islands. Entranced by the beauty of the island, they named it "Ihla Formosa," meaning "beautiful island." Using the island as a port to provision their ships, the Portuguese made no effort to colonize Formosa.

Meanwhile, a Japanese settlement in An-Ping (now the port of Tainan) served as a port of call in Japan's trade route. The Japanese merchants named the island Taiwan, or "big bay."

Current Chinese rulers on Taiwan assert that Taiwanese people who call themselves Formosan deny their native identity and are anti-Chinese because

The author would like to thank the Reverend Jonah Chang, Mr. Leon Chang, and Mrs. Mary Chang, who were principal sources of information for this chapter. Sociocultural background and immigration information was provided by the former staff associate of the Formosan Association for Public Affairs (FAPA), Dr. Marc J. Cohen.

they refer to themselves by a foreign (Portuguese) name. Hypocritically, these same rulers use the Japanese name Taiwan without problem. No one would think to call Taiwan (or Formosa) by its Chinese name: "Pakkan-Tao," or "island of the northern anchorages."

Foreign as their origins may be, the names Taiwan and Formosa have remained popular and are used interchangeably in this narrative in reference to the indigenous people of the island. The name "Republic of China," on the other hand, is used in this narrative to designate the ruling Kuomintang (KMT) regime, or Nationalist Chinese government, on Taiwan.

Taiwan's long history of oppression by "outsiders" served to strengthen Taiwanese identity, especially in the United States where freedom of speech could be practiced by the largest population of Formosans outside of Taiwan.

In a nutshell, Taiwan's history of oppression includes Dutch rule in the first decade of the seventeenth century, when natives were forced to produce such crops as sugar cane. In 1662 the Han general of the Ming Dynasty, Cheng Ch'eng Kung (later known as Koxinga), drove out the Dutch and "conquered" Formosa. In other accounts mitigating his victory, Koxinga was defeated and kicked out of China by the Manchus (whose rule became known as Ch'ing Dynasty) and forced to flee to Taiwan. In a preview of what was to happen in 1949 with General Chiang Kai-shek, the Han general declared himself emperor of all of China and set Tainan in southern Taiwan as his capital, declaring that he would one day recapture the mainland. He never did.

In 1895, by the stroke of a pen in the Sino-Japanese Treaty, Taiwan was given to Japan. After World War II, by another penstroke, Taiwan suddenly belonged to the Republic of China. In 1949 when the Republic of China lost its civil war to Communist forces, its leaders, led by Chiang Kai-shek, fled in exile to Taiwan and imposed martial law, declaring they would one day recover the mainland. Thirty-seven years later in the summer of 1987, the Nationalist Chinese government officially "lifted" martial law—a cosmetic measure since most of the martial law provisions were built into the new National Security Law.

ROOTS OF THE TAIWANESE CHRISTIAN IDENTITY

Throughout the changes from one oppressive government to another, Formosan leaders managed to foster a Protestant spirit inspired by early Dutch missionaries. This spirit is reflected in the "Homeland Theology" paper developed between 1972 and 1978 by leaders of Taiwan's Protestant churches. This statement of self-determination was divided into three sections, each expressing a vital idea: "Fate of our Homeland," "Our Appeal to the People of the World," and "Human Rights Declaration."

The Nationalist Chinese rulers on Taiwan saw "Homeland Theology" as a threat to their authoritarian rule. They branded it Communist propaganda, confiscated Bibles written in the four romanized versions of the Taiwanese dialect (Mandarin is the official language of the Republic of China, although roughly 70 percent of the population is of Taiwanese ancestry), and imprisoned many Protestant church leaders, including Dr. Chun-Ming Kao, general secretary of the Taiwan Presbyterian Church.

The persecution of these Formosan Christian leaders had repercussions not only for the development of the Taiwanese American United Methodist Church but for the general church as well. In 1980 human rights violations in Taiwan reached the attention of the General Conference of The United Methodist Church.

In early 1980 the Reverend Thomas Tai, pastor of First Formosan United Methodist church, collected funds in order to send a human rights fact-finding team to Taiwan. Team members, selected for their history of human rights activism, included the Reverend Lloyd Wake, the Reverend Jonah Chang, the Reverend John Moore (who was a member of the General Board of Church and Society), and Mrs. Ruth Prudente (whose husband was a prisoner of conscience in the Philippines under President Ferdinand Marcos). Except for Mrs. Prudente, the team members were all elected delegates from the California-Nevada Annual Conference to the 1980 General Conference.

On April 20, 1980, the team members made their motion on the floor of General Conference to adopt the resolution "Formosan Churches (Presbyterian) under Persecution and Political Terror." Mr. Chang's report that the Reverend C. M. Kao had been arrested that very day added dramatic impact to the motion, which was passed by the 1980 General Conference. The motion resolved to "strongly support the struggle of the Formosan people for their human rights and religious freedom and their right to participate fully in the political processes of their country." The General Conference also approved the sending of a cablegram to President Chiang Ching Kuo of the Republic of China, expressing deep concern over Dr. Kao's arrest, and to the Presbyterian Church of Taiwan, expressing wholehearted support of its imprisoned general secretary.[1]

The tie that bound together the Taiwanese identity all over the world was and still is the common desire to see human rights restored in Taiwan. The Reverend Wu-Tong Huang, former general secretary of the Taiwan Presbyterian Church, touchingly captured the yearning of Taiwanese people all over the world for justice for Taiwan in his song "Lamentation of the Wanderer":

> We, who wandering, praying, hope for home restored,
> Trust that freedom will come to us someday.

IMMIGRATION HISTORY

Immediately after World War II until 1965, emigrants from Taiwan were mainly made up of students who were able to find jobs and therefore stay in the United States after their studies.

At the end of 1965 an immigration quota of 20,000 Chinese per year was declared. Since the United States did not recognize—politically or culturally—the People's Republic of China, the Chinese immigration quota applied only to people from Taiwan. In December 1972, when the first Formosan United Methodist congregation was being established, the Republic of China was kicked out of the United Nations. This sign of political instability sparked a desire among many Taiwanese to emigrate, causing a steady increase in the Taiwanese population in the United States.

In 1979 the United States finally recognized the government of the People's Republic of China (PRC) and allowed immigrants from that country to be included in the quota, so that Taiwanese were then in competition with mainland Chinese for inclusion in the quota of 20,000 (Taiwanese immigration still dominated, however). In 1981 the quotas were separated, and 20,000 PRC Chinese were allowed to immigrate along with 20,000 Taiwanese.

By 1987 an estimated 300,000 Taiwanese resided in the United States. (An accurate count is impossible because the federal government refuses to differentiate between Taiwanese Americans and Chinese Americans in its census and government policies.)

EARLY FORMOSAN UNITED METHODIST MINISTRY, 1966 TO 1975

In 1966 a young Presbyterian pastor working part-time at Sycamore Congregational Church, a Japanese church across the bay from San Francisco in the El Cerrito hills, attempted to minister to the Taiwanese in the Bay Area. The Reverend Jonah Jui-Hsiung Chang organized monthly prayer meetings that attracted an average of thirty people—mostly students—from a seventy-five miles radius.

A year later, serving a full-time appointment as a supply pastor at Christ Methodist Church in Fresno, California, Pastor Chang continued searching out Formosans in nearby communities and organizing regular meetings, even managing to organize a meeting in Santa Cruz 150 miles away.

Although over seventy Taiwanese American churches and fellowship groups had sprung up around the country by 1985, no Taiwanese support base had yet been established. As a result, Japanese American churches were called upon to lend financial and spiritual support to the fledgling Formosan ministry.

Utilizing the support base offered by the Los Angeles Japanese church, Centenary United Methodist Church (the Reverend Peter Chen, pastor), Chang organized a Formosan congregation during his summer vacation in 1970. This attempt at establishing a Formosan United Methodist ministry in Southern California met with limited success. The congregation grew and later became Presbyterian because, some Formosans perceived, United Methodist leaders in the Southern California-Arizona Annual Conference failed to aggressively pursue and support the church. At the end of his summer vacation Chang left the newly formed fellowship and returned to Fresno.

In 1971 the largest known gathering, at the time, of Taiwanese in the United States took place at Sycamore Congregational Church. Over three hundred Formosans took part in a celebration of the lunar New Year, indicating that the San Francisco Bay Area harbored a sizeable and growing Taiwanese community.

By that time, Chang had become a full member of the California-Nevada Annual Conference. Appointed to Buena Vista United Methodist Church, a Japanese church in the Bay Area, in July 1971, he began acquainting himself with the new Formosan community.

Several Taiwanese families and individuals expressed interest in supporting a congregation and regularly attended afternoon Taiwanese services at Buena Vista. These people, including Leon Chang and family, Johnson Su and family, Jackson Ting and family, and Carla Chang (later Mrs. Carla Chen), became the founders of the Formosan United Methodist Church.

Afternoon services were inconvenient for many families, so in the spring of 1973 morning worship services were established at Epworth United Methodist Church in Berkeley (the Reverend William W. Dew, Jr., pastor). These morning services maintained a regular, growing attendance, while afternoon services seemed to attract only a few regulars. For over a year the afternoon services were moved every few months as the congregation's leaders experimented with different locations in an attempt to identify large Formosan communities.

The first afternoon service was held at Aldersgate United Methodist Church in Palo Alto (the Reverend Alpha Takagi, pastor). After only a few months, services were moved to Pine United Methodist Church, San Francisco (the Reverend Jiro Mizuno, pastor), where they stayed for several months. When this proved unsuccessful, services were moved one last time to Carlmont United Methodist Church in San Carlos (the Reverend Donald R. Fellers, pastor) for six months.

Based on the advice of an Easter Sunday guest preacher in 1974, the Epworth congregation's leaders decided to consolidate morning and afternoon worship services at Hayward First United Methodist Church (the Reverend Harold Hewitt, pastor). That summer the leaders of the congregation began looking for a permanent pastor.

Hayward Formosan United Methodist Fellowship

A Formosan Indigenous Community Developer (ICD) committee was formed under the guidance of Chang, who was a member of the General Board of Global Ministries that administered the program. In August the newly formed committee contacted the Reverend Thomas C. N. Tai, a doctoral candidate at Brite Divinity School, Texas Christian University, Fort Worth, Texas. The committee asked him to become the half-time ICD of the Taiwanese community in the Bay Area and, in the other half-time, serve as "organizing pastor" of the congregation.

Tai accepted the positions, so in the fall the Epworth congregation moved to Hayward and became the first Formosan United Methodist fellowship in the United States to have a permanent mailing address and an identifiable location. Tai had not yet finished his dissertation, so he did not move to the Bay Area for full-time work until January 1975. In the meantime, he ministered to the Formosan community by commuting between Fort Worth and San Francisco about every other week.

On July 7, 1975, at the California-Nevada Annual Conference in Stockton, Tai was recognized as a probationary member of The United Methodist Church and was appointed by Bishop R. Marvin Stuart as a part-time pastor of the Formosan United Methodist Fellowship of the San Francisco Bay Area and a part-time Formosan ICD.

On August 10 that year, under the administration of the Reverend John Moore, district superintendent of the Bayview District, and Bishop Stuart, the Formosan United Methodist Church of the San Francisco Bay Area was chartered as the first Taiwanese United Methodist church in the United States. It was, in fact, the first Taiwanese United Methodist church in the world, since the approximately twenty Methodist churches in Taiwan were Chinese (of the Republic of China) and not Taiwanese.

On its tenth anniversary celebration in 1985, the Formosan United Methodist Church of the Bay Area published a history of the founding of the church. Mrs. Chris Lin and other church leaders invited Rev. Tai to pastor their church so he gave up a good job as hospital chaplain elsewhere in the U.S. to come to the Bay Area. Faced with many hardships in getting the church organized, he and a few leaders established the church. The congregation has moved to San Leandro, California, and the current minister is the Reverend Timothy Chuang.

NEW DIRECTIONS, 1975

When Tai began his work at Formosan United Methodist Church, his salary came partially from the ICD Program and partially from the California-

Nevada Annual Conference. Bayview district superintendent John Moore helped pool the financial support so that the church could offer Tai a full-time salary. As the new church grew, however, an assistant was needed to help in reaching Formosans in the community. In 1976 the ICD committee hired Mr. Lung Chen, a candidate for diaconal ministry, as the director of the Formosan ICD. Tai continued to serve as supervising pastor.

Park Presidio United Methodist Church Formosan Ministry

While nurturing the Formosan United Methodist Church in Hayward, Tai also began working with the Formosan community in San Francisco. On February 1, 1976, a Taiwanese fellowship group was established at Park Presidio United Methodist Church (the Reverend Travis Campbell, pastor). In 1978, to relieve Tai's burden of caring for two congregations, Park Presidio hired an ordained Taiwan Holiness Church minister, the Reverend Frank Yang, to do the church's Formosan language ministry.

The following year the congregation voted to remain under the administrative care of Park Presidio United Methodist Church and not become a separate charter, and Yang was appointed the church's associate pastor with responsibility for Formosan language ministry.

From 1978 until 1982 Yang worked without United Methodist recognition and credit. Finally appointed a local pastor in 1982, his Taiwan Holiness Church order was recognized in 1983, and he was granted a probationary membership. In 1985 his United Methodist order was recognized, and he was granted full membership in the Conference.

South Bay Formosan Ministry

The Bay Area Formosan community was growing rapidly by 1979 and was spreading southward with the burgeoning computer industry. Some members of the Hayward church had to drive up to an hour and a half to get to church—a daunting feat in the face of a dawning energy crisis. At a September 1979 charge conference, the congregation voted to divide into two and start a congregation in the South Bay area, also known as Silicon Valley, approximately fifty miles south of San Francisco.

The South Bay group began meeting in the first week of November 1979 at Trinity United Methodist Church in Sunnyvale (the Reverend John Fugitt, pastor); the other group met at Epworth in Berkeley (the Reverend David Slorp, pastor). Tai pastored both congregations, alternating in the South Bay and James Peng (a seminary student at the Pacific School of Religion) until a permanent pastor, former Taiwan Holiness preacher Donald Liu, was hired.

From the very beginning this congregation was self-supporting, having in its membership a majority of the active leaders of the old, undivided church.

It was natural that these leaders would want to continue their relationship with The United Methodist Church since their previous experience with the denomination had been favorable. However, the San Jose district superintendent and the California-Nevada bishop met their enthusiasm with ambivalence, making it impossible for the new congregation to gain United Methodist recognition.

In 1980, determined to be United Methodist or nothing else, the South Bay congregation spurned overtures from the Evangelical and Presbyterian denominations and became independent, naming itself Canaan Christian Church. In a commonly practiced independent church ordination process, Liu was approved and ordained by an ordination committee consisting of three pastors commissioned from different denominations. Many of the church's leaders were forced to revoke their membership in The United Methodist Church to become independent; these individuals include Mr. Chris Lin, Mr. Patrick Huang, Mr. Ted Huang, Mr. Ki-Sek Teng, Dr. Lung Chi Lee, and Mr. Chieh-San Huang.

Ironically, the church eventually proved to be stronger and larger than its parent, with over three hundred members in 1987.

Despite the rift with The United Methodist Church, Canaan Christian Church still maintained lingering ties with United Methodists. The congregation purchased the site and facilities of the former La Trinidad United Methodist Church in Mountain View, which had died from lack of membership, and members retained friendships with Formosan United Methodists in the North Bay.

East Bay Formosan Fellowship

In October 1980 Tai and the First Formosan United Methodist Church moved to Rockridge Memorial United Methodist Church in Oakland, where a white congregation was losing membership and welcomed the new church. The new, more urban location, was essential to the church's growth, especially since its membership tended to be new immigrants.

A faction of the congregation wanted to remain in Berkeley, ostensibly to cultivate a student membership from the University of California nearby; but primarily, the traditional Taiwanese leaders of the congregation felt the Formosan United Methodist Church was not adequately addressing the concerns of the Taiwanese community, especially concerns for human rights in Taiwan.

Members of the congregation felt that the Kaohsiung Incident of December 1979 was the catalyst for these strong divisions in the Formosan United Methodist Church. This emotional incident, in which students and human rights activists clashed with government-sponsored counter demonstrators at a human rights rally at Kaohsiung University (in central Taiwan), led to the arrest of

Taiwan Presbyterian Church leaders and other human rights leaders. Many felt the Formosan United Methodist church was not demonstrating enough solidarity with these persecuted church and human rights leaders. On the basis of this perceived philosophical difference, the splinter group formed a new congregation that, in October 1980, began meeting at Berkeley United Methodist Church (the Reverend Grant Hagiya, pastor).

In January 1982 the new congregation moved to Walnut Creek, where a large population of Taiwanese professionals lived. The congregation used the facilities at First United Methodist Church of Walnut Creek (the Reverend Douglas Hayward, pastor) and called itself Taiwanese Christian Church. In mid-March 1985 the congregation hired the Reverend George Lee, a Taiwan Presbyterian Church minister pastoring a Taiwanese United Church of Christ church in Seattle.

In December 1986 the congregation voted to join The United Methodist Church, agreeing to meet the stipulation that it maintain a membership of at least fifty adults. The congregation received its charter as a Methodist congregation in 1987. Currently, the pastor is the Reverend Benjamin Wu.

FELLOWSHIPS THAT GOT AWAY

As in Los Angeles when Jonah Chang tried to establish a Formosan ministry, Dallas and New York were sites of a large and growing population of Formosans in the late 1970s. And as with the Los Angeles fellowship, the Dallas and New York United Methodist–related fellowships ultimately turned away from the denomination.

Chang helped establish the Dallas fellowship in 1978. But, he claimed, because of lack of aggressive leadership and support from the Northern Texas Annual Conference, the congregation voted in 1985 not to become United Methodist. Under the leadership of the Reverend James Chi, at one time a United Methodist candidate for full connection, the Dallas Taiwanese Christian Church was self-supporting from its birth and continued to grow after rejecting the United Methodist affiliation.

Similarly, although some observers would claim there were other reasons, the Formosan congregation in New York, Zion Taiwanese Christian Church (the Reverend Ito Chang, pastor), voted in the early 1980s not to become United Methodist.

FORMOSAN UNITED METHODIST WOMEN

The purpose of the Hu Lu Tso (Fu Nü Tsu), or women's group, was traditionally to nurture spiritual growth through Bible study and prayer. The

Hu Lu Tso in the early Formosan Bay Area Fellowship, however, was organized mainly to assign lunch duty. About a year after the Formosan United Methodist Church was chartered, its leaders decided to offer lunch after worship services each Sunday to help foster fellowship among church members. A Hu Lu Tso composed mainly of wives was formed to assign two-family teams to cook lunch for the congregation. Mrs. Jane Chang, first president of the Hu Lu Tso, besides assigning lunch duties, would also sometimes invite a speaker to lead discussions or give advice on such topics as cooking, makeup, and family education. When the church moved to Epworth in 1979, the Hu Lu Tso was dissolved because there was no longer a need to serve lunch.

While the contribution of the women's group was important to the growth and life of the church, it was also traditional in nature—cooking, cleaning, babysitting, and Sunday school teaching. One woman notably gave integral leadership to the early Formosan congregation, and later to the Formosan United Methodist Church, that was not traditional for a Formosan woman and was rarely acknowledged.

Mary Mei-Hwa Chang worked alongside her husband, Jonah Chang, as he worked to establish the Formosan congregation at Buena Vista United Methodist Church. She kept records of attendance and the Order of Worship, she played the organ for worship services, and she served refreshments after the service.

When Chang became director of Asian American Ministries of the Western Jurisdiction in 1973, his new duties left him little time to continue local church ministry to the Formosan congregation. While pastor of Buena Vista, his Formosan ministry was an extension of his Japanese ministry. With no other Formosan pastor available to share the ministerial burden, the job fell to Mrs. Chang, a 1958 graduate of Tiong-Tai Seng Keng Su-in (Chung Tai Shung-Ching Schu-Yuan), the four-year Central Taiwan Bible College.

From March to August, 1974 Mrs. Chang assumed the job of Christian Worker of the Taiwanese congregation. Her duties included giving the sermon at Epworth when Chang was out of town, songleading, choir directing, playing the organ for worship, initiating the potluck lunch, and visiting new and potential members. She received a stipend of fifty dollars per month (from funds received from Sunday offerings) for her six-month term as Christian Worker. Her work involved three months of ministry to the congregations at Epworth in the morning, plus Pine United Methodist Church in the afternoon, and three months of ministry to the congregations at Epworth in the morning, plus San Carlos in the afternoon. Her heavy responsibilities, added to her new full-time job outside of the church, took their toll on her energy, so that after six months she was unable to continue.

At this point the leaders of the congregation decided that they needed to hire a full-time minister, and they began their search.

SUNDAY SCHOOL AND BILINGUAL MINISTRY

Often used as an indicator of a church's vitality, the strength of Sunday school and youth programs of the immigrant church also served to indicate the church's degree of assimilation into the mainstream society.

Ministering to the children of the Taiwanese church members was easy at first. The Taiwanese population in the 1960s was primarily composed of college graduates and their young families, so the early congregation had two ministries—adults and children. Adults attended Taiwanese worship service, and children attended Sunday school—a combination of playtime, crafts, singing, and Bible storytelling. When the congregation began meeting at Epworth in the morning in 1973, the children joined the host church's Sunday school classes, which were divided by grade level.

When the congregation became the Formosan United Methodist Church and moved to Hayward, it began its own Sunday school, taught by Mrs. Chin S. Yang for approximately three years. The children were still young and could easily be separated into two groups—infants and school-aged. As the children got older and new immigrant children joined, Sunday school became more complex. In 1976 Mr. Zee Iuan Kau was nominated its first principal, to serve as coordinator of the Sunday School program.

By 1977 the age levels had become so varied, with some children having grown to high school level, that a youth ministry became necessary. In July 1977 Mr. James Peng, a student at the Pacific School of Religion in Berkeley, was hired as the first youth meeting director. Each subsequent division of the church seemed to cut the youth groups into smaller pieces, making programs difficult to implement at first.

In the mid-1980s a new element was emerging to add to the dynamics of the growing church. Taiwanese American youth were graduating from college yet were still attending Sunday school because worship services were conducted in Taiwanese, a language they could no longer understand; alternatively, some were dropping out of the church altogether. As of this writing, the various United Methodist and formerly United Methodist-related Formosan churches across the country are experimenting with different methods of bilingual ministry, preparing to meet the challenge presented by second-generation Taiwanese Americans.

The next and final phase of bilingual ministry—ministry to Taiwanese and their non-Taiwanese spouses—promises to bring the Taiwanese church into the American mainstream, and at the same time promises to bring the American mainstream to an awareness of the richness of the Taiwanese culture. As of this writing, the oldest of the Taiwanese American second generation has only begun to reach marriage age. Their future, like that of the newly born church, rests in the strength of their Formosan identity.

FORMOSAN UNITED METHODIST MINISTERS

Although they are not serving Formosan churches and are not mentioned elsewhere in this narrative, the following United Methodist Formosan pastors have contributed their talents to The United Methodist Church: the Reverend Norman Kao, the Reverend David Chen, The Reverend Tong Liu (has served primarily Japanese churches), the Reverend Peter Chen (born in Taiwan but raised in Japan; has served primarily Japanese churches), and the Reverend Yung S. Chen (the first Formosan to chair the National Federation of Asian American United Methodists, elected January 1987).

FORMOSAN CHURCHES IN THE UNITED STATES

In 1985 the interdenominational Taiwanese Christian Church Council in North America (TCCCNA) published the results of a comprehensive survey of Taiwanese Protestant churches in the United States. The resulting book by W. T. Huang, written in Chinese, is titled *A History of the Development of Taiwanese Christian Churches in North America*. Though not entirely complete for every entry, the book gives details of churches, fellowships, and Bible study groups in the United States that identified themselves as Taiwanese.

For a brief overview of the denominational composition of the Formosan Protestant church in the United States, results of the survey are summarized below.[2]

Independent Taiwanese Churches in American	22
The Taiwanese Presbyterian Churches in America	21
Evangelical Formosan Church in America	10
Taiwanese Reformed Churches in America	6
The Lutheran Taiwanese Churches in America	3
The United Methodist Taiwanese Church	3
Taiwanese Christian Bible Study Groups and Fellowships	5
TOTAL	70

NOTES

1. For the full text of the resolution and related debate, see *Journal of the 1980 General Conference* (Evanston, Ill.: General Council on Finance and Administration, The United Methodist Church), pp. 864-65, 510-11, respectively.

2. Individual church names and information about them are available from the TCCCNA, 6501 York Boulevard, Los Angeles, CA 90042.

C H A P T E R 3

TRIALS AND TRIUMPHS:
History of Korean
United Methodist Churches

Key Ray Chong and
Myong Gul Son

In January 1903, 101 Koreans arrived in Honolulu. They were the first immigrants sent to America by the Korean government. Many subsequently followed suit. After World War II, Koreans started going abroad in droves: to Argentina in 1957, to Brazil in 1961, to Canada in 1964, to Paraguay in 1965, and to Uruguay in 1972. The Ministry of Foreign Affairs of the Republic of Korea reported that as of June 1986 there were 2,008,445 Korean emigrants, over half of them—1,024,927—living in the United States and the rest in Japan, Canada, and South America.[1] Koreans are still coming to the United States in great numbers. In 1986 alone, almost 40,000 Koreans (out of a total of 400,000 immigrants) entered this country, a figure trailing only those for Mexicans and Filipinos.

Besides, another two million Koreans are living in Communist countries such as China and the Soviet Union. In China alone, there are about 1.5 million Koreans today.[2] They had left for those strange lands to enjoy political, economic, and religious freedom, especially when the Japanese annexed Korea in 1910. For the very same reasons the Koreans had also gone to Hawaii and several other North and South American countries.

The primary purpose of this chapter is to present a brief history of Korean Methodists who settled in the United States. The secondary purpose is to discuss why they came and how they lived in the new country. By so doing, we hope to understand the suffering and success of the Korean immigrants in a strange and sometimes hostile land.

CHRISTIANITY IN KOREA

By way of introduction, let us begin with Christianity in Korea. In 1592 two hundred Koreans were baptized by a Catholic missionary in Korea, and later another two thousand in Japan. Many Korean prisoners of war taken to Japan had received baptism during captivity, but most of them were executed along with Japanese Christians during the anti-Christian campaign of 1614.[3] Thus no survivors returned to Korea, nor did the seed of Christian gospel grow in the hearts of their compatriots back home.

Christianity was again introduced to Korea in 1641. Korean officials, while visiting China as members of the annual tribute mission, picked up a Christian book entitled the *True Doctrine of the Heavenly Lord*, written by Matteo Ricci, a Jesuit missionary to Peking. When they returned home, they took with them this first Christian book. Since it was illegal to bring such a book into Korea, they did it secretly.[4] The Christian gospel slowly began spreading. Its growth was fostered by the efforts of a noted Korean Confucian scholar, Yi Seung-hun, who had studied about it in China and returned home in 1784 with more Christian books.[5]

Until 1884 Christianity grew slowly and secretly in Korea because the Yi government banned it and supported Confucianism. Converts therefore went through numerous trials and tribulations: indiscriminate killing and arbitrary imprisonment at the hands of their government. In 1836, for example, over two hundred Catholic adherents were killed in an effort to wipe out the Christian religion in Korea.[6]

In the midst of this trying time, in 1876, two American missionaries, John Ross and John McIntyre, converted four visiting Korean scholars in Peking. The Reverend John Ross later baptized So Sang-yun and Yi Eung-chan in Seoul. The first four converts, led by So Sang-yun, translated part of the New Testament into Korean and returned to Korea with it.[7] To bolster Christian evangelism in Korea, two more American missionaries went there in 1885: Horace Grant Underwood, a Northern Presbyterian, and Henry Gerhart Appenzeller, a Northern Methodist.[8] They laid the foundation for Presbyterianism and Methodism in Korea.

Methodism was introduced into Korea in 1885. The United States–Korean Treaty of Amity and Commerce of 1882 had opened the Hermit Kingdom to the Western world. According to the treaty, American Methodists and others were allowed to come and work in Korea without government persecution such as the Korean Catholics had experienced. The Korean Catholic martyrs paved the way for Protestant work in Korea. Americans preached the gospel of Jesus Christ to those who had persecuted their predecessors. But American Methodist missionaries also emphasized education, medicine, and social welfare to improve the quality of life for the Koreans, both spiritually and physically. Many Korean converts later became leaders in those fields. In contrast, Presbyterians concentrated on local church development. Thus within a century or so, Presbyterianism and Methodism became the two largest Christian denominations in Korea, first and second in membership, respectively.

48

THE TRIAL PERIOD, 1903 TO 1945

Immigration to Hawaii

Now the Lord said to Abram, "Go from your country and your kindred and your father's house to the land that I will show you." (Genesis 12:1 RSV).

Since Korean Methodists had benefited considerably from Christian civilization in the form of modern education and medicine, many of them went to Hawaii in 1903 as the first batch of immigrants. Members of the Naeri Methodist Church in Inchon, the first Methodist church in Korea, were among the first group of Korean immigrants to go to Hawaii. In 1902 the East-West Development Company of Hawaii wanted to replace Japanese laborers on sugar plantations with Koreans because it had suffered from frequent labor disputes with the numerically strong Japanese. The Japanese comprised 73.6 percent of the total population in Hawaii as of 1902, that is, 31,129 of 42,242. When the company advertised the recruitment of laborers, Korean Methodists responded most positively. This was largely because the Sugar Plantation Association in Hawaii had asked American Methodist missionaries in Korea, such as Henry G. Appenzeller and George H. Jones, to encourage their congregations to go to Hawaii for a better life. As a result, 101 Korean immigrants reached Hawaii in January 1903. Among them were 71 adults and 30 children. Fifty-eight adults were professed Christians, 20 from the Naeri Methodist Church in Inchon and the rest, 38, from neighboring churches.[9]

Clearly, a close cooperation existed between American sugar companies and missionary groups and/or between American missionaries and Korean immigrants. Such symbiotic relationships were well demonstrated in F. H. Harrington's *God, Mammon and Japanese* (1914). In fact, Jones recruited his Korean followers to go to Hawaii for good pay, good educational opportunities, good housing, and good medical care. His Christian followers naturally took advantage of this golden opportunity since they were at the bottom of Korean society. Since 65 percent of them were illiterate, they were eager to provide education for their children, which was a passport to success in Korea in those days.[10] In short, they tried to realize their lifelong dreams in Hawaii through American Methodist missionaries.

There were other reasons for the Koreans to go to Hawaii. In the wake of the Sino-Japanese War of 1895, the Chinese lost control of Korea, and their defeat paved the way for Japanese suzerainty there. Soon thereafter, the Japanese reduced Korea virtually to nonentity status, although it had maintained the public status of semi-independent nation. When this occurred, the livelihood of the Korean people went from bad to worse. Furthermore, Koreans were victimized by internal catastrophes such as the Tonghak Rebellion of 1895 and subsequently a series of natural disasters such as flood and drought. The Tonghak Rebellion, a proto-nationalist movement, attempted to eliminate political corruption from within and Western influence from without. During the Tonghak Rebellion, Japanese troops played a big role in crushing the rebels. When natural disasters hit the country several years in a row, many Koreans found it increasingly difficult to live in their country. Being aware of these crises, considerable numbers of Korean Methodists left for the new world to enjoy religious, economic, and political freedom, just as the Puritans had done two centuries earlier.

Like the Puritans, the Korean Methodists were equally eager to practice their religion. During the voyage to Hawaii, Kim Yi-chae, a layperson, preached to his countrymen on board. When the Koreans settled down in Hawaii at the end of 1903, they received the Reverend Hong Seung-ha, the first Korean Methodist minister in Hawaii, sent by the Naeri Methodist Church in Inchon. He conducted the first service in Hawaii for the Korean congregation with the help of American Methodist officials. By December 1904, under the leadership of Hong, $300 was raised for the building funds plus $1,000 in donations from American supporters. With this money the new building, located at Emma Street, Honolulu, was purchased. This was the beginning of Korean Methodism in Hawaii. The building today houses the oldest Korean Methodist church in Hawaii, known as Christ United Methodist Church of Honolulu (which was later pastored by the Reverend Yi Eung-kyun [Eung Kyun Lee]).

Subsequently, many more Korean Methodist churches were established in Hawaii. In the period 1903 to 1905, 7,225 Koreans came to Hawaii on sixty-five different ships, according to the records of the U.S. Immigration and Naturalization Service. As of 1911 there were twenty Korean Methodist churches; by 1916 there were thirty-one churches and thirty-five mission stations with a total membership of over 2,800 throughout the Hawaiian Islands. This growth rate was phenomenal in view of the low numbers of Korean immigrants during these years. There were only 7,226 Korean immigrants to Hawaii before 1905: 6,048 men, 637 women, and 54 children; after 1905, a new law banned practically all Asian immigrants except for Filipinos, and the Korean population decreased drastically due to fewer incoming Koreans and the death or return home of existing Korean immigrants. The picture was equally bleak in the continental United States; during the same period there were only seven mission stations and 452 members on the mainland,[11] all of whom had moved there from Hawaii. By 1910 there were only 4,000 Koreans in the United States.

Why did Koreans respond positively to the message of the Methodist Church in Hawaii? First, unlike the Japanese and Chinese who had brought with them Shinto and Buddhism, the Koreans did not have strong religious beliefs, although they had strongly adhered to secular Confucian teaching.

Because of this, they were receptive to the gospel of Jesus Christ and accepted it for spiritual enrichment. Second, more than 50 percent of Korean immigrants in Hawaii were already professed Christians. Thus Christianity was not at all alien to them. Third, the Korean Methodists were much more familiar with Christianity compared to other ethnic groups in Hawaii since their church had long taught them how to sing hymns and how to read the Bible through the worship service back in Korea. At the Korean church English was also taught, not only to educate Korean immigrants but also to improve their quality of life in the new country.

The Koreans turned to the church for other reasons. They went to Hawaii in hopes of living in a paradise on earth, but instead they found a hard life there. They worked six days a week and during the harvest seven days in a row. Their working hours were long. For example, cooks on a sugar plantation got up at three in the morning and prepared meals. Workers got up at 5:00 and ate breakfast. By 5:30 they were ready to go to work. At 6:00 sharp they began their daily work. Except for the thirty-minute lunch break, they worked ten hours straight every day. Their wages were low; an average male worker earned from $16 to $18 a month—65 to 70 cents a day (in the case of women, 60 to 65 cents a day).[12] Average American workers on the mainland at that time earned at least $1 a day.

The workers were treated badly. They were not permitted to use their personal name at work; they were given an ID number card instead of a name tag. Once they started working, they were not allowed to stand up or stretch out their body, nor were they allowed to talk or smoke while working. When those rules were violated, they were severely whipped or beaten by foremen. Despite such harsh treatment, no one could protest or complain. After work they retired to living quarters built like army barracks. They slept on wooden beds and often on a wooden floor with only a blanket for cover. Four people would be crammed into each room. However physically exhausted, they would hardly go to sleep during the hot summer nights because there was no cooling or ventilation system in the room; breathing stuffy, polluted air made it difficult to have a good night's sleep. Consequently, many contracted tuberculosis and died.[13] Living conditions for the Koreans were so bad that in 1905 T. H. Yun, vice minister of foreign affairs of Korea, visited Hawaii and expressed grave concern for the plight of his countrymen. But nothing changed their miserable conditions.[14]

Under these circumstances, they were helpless and desperate. Out of frustration, many Koreans led a decadent life, squandering money for gambling, drinking, and prostitutes. Since most of them had no family to take care of, they saved no money at all. When the church spoke of the good news of Jesus Christ to these men, they responded quickly and positively. They accepted the Christian faith more willingly than had any other ethnic minority group in Hawaii. For example, as of 1911 there were in Hawaii eight Japanese-speaking Methodist congregations, compared to twenty-two Korean-speaking ones, even though the Japanese outnumbered the Koreans. Initially two different American mission groups were interested in evangelizing the Koreans in Hawaii. But after 1910 only the Methodist mission continued to concentrate on the Korean ministry.[15]

The early Korean immigrants also turned to Christianity for political reasons. The Methodist Church in Hawaii was instrumental in raising their political consciousness. In fact, the overtly political activities of Methodist leaders attracted many patriotic Koreans to church. For example, the Reverend Hong Seung-ha played a leading role in organizing the New People Society (*sinmin hoe*) in late 1903, the first Korean political organization in America. The founding father of the Republic of Korea, Dr. Yi Seung-man (better known as Syngman Rhee), organized the Comrade Society (*tongji ho*) in 1921 with the help of the Methodist Church.[16] When Rhee became the first president of the Republic of Korea in 1948, many of his first cabinet members had developed political or personal relations with him through the Methodist Church in Hawaii or the mainland United States (which demonstrates that Korean Methodists in Hawaii effectively did not separate church and state).

Mainland Korean Methodists

Against the background of these Hawaiian experiences, let us deal with Korean Methodists on the mainland; the discussion will focus on several churches.

San Francisco

As of August 1903, there were only twenty-five Koreans in San Francisco, most of them from Hawaii. By 1905, however, there were fifty Koreans in San Francisco. On October 8, 1905, the Korean Mission Society was established under the leadership of evangelist Mun Kyung-ho. On July 15, 1906, the San Francisco Korean Methodist Church was opened by another evangelist, Bang Hwa-chung. On December 16 of the same year, the church building was dedicated, and the Reverend Yang Chu-sam (better know as J. S. Ryang) was appointed the first full-time pastor by Dr. C. F. Reid (1849–1915), one of the first Southern Methodist missionaries to Korea.

Korean Methodists promoted political as well as religious activism, in support of Korean independence, now threatened by the Japanese. From 1908 to 1909 there were a series of assassination attempts on the lives of collaborators with the Japanese. On March 23, 1908, two young Koreans in San Francisco—Chang In-hwan and Chun Myung-wun—gunned down D. W. Stevens (the American minister and unofficial advisor to the Japanese governor-general in Korea) at the Oakland train station. Reflecting the view of the United States government toward the situation, as expressed in the Taft-Katsura Agreement of 1905, Stevens favored Japanese rule over Korea. When the two Koreans were put on trial at court, Shin Heung-wu, a Methodist studying for his doctorate at the University of Southern California, served as the court-designated interpreter for their defense. Chang and Chun received moral and material help from members of the Korean Methodist church during the trial. They were found guilty, but because of the legal defense provided by the Methodist Church in San Francisco, their lives were spared.

Methodist support for the Korean nationalist movement continued. When An Chang-ho, a prominent Nationalist leader, established the Talent Cultivation Society (*heungsa dan*) in San Francisco on May 13, 1913, with the purpose of promoting the political and economic interests of Koreans, the San Francisco Korean Methodist Church was more than willing to cooperate with him; in February 1915 it allowed him to use their building as his office.[17]

In the period 1915 to 1928, the San Francisco Methodist Church grew financially and spiritually under the leadership of the Reverend Yang Chu-sam. By 1928 it became the first Korean Methodist church in the mainland United States. It was independently owned and operated by the Koreans, having raised $18,000 from its members, and it received a substantial amount of building funds from the Methodist Mission. In honor of Yang, who had served as the first full-fledged pastor of the San Francisco Korean Methodist Church, the name of the church was changed to Bishop Yang Memorial Church in San Francisco after he was appointed the first Korean general superintendent (later bishop) in 1930.[18] This church, formerly a member of the Oriental Provisional Mission, is currently well and alive; it has been led by such pastors as the late Reverend Charles Song and Dr. Cha Won-tae. Encouraged by this development, a group of Koreans across the San Francisco Bay organized another Methodist church in Oakland in 1914. This church has also been led by many pastors, such as Dr. Kim Chan-su and the Reverend Kim Kwang-jin.

Los Angeles

As elsewhere, the Korean Methodist church in Los Angeles was small at the turn of the century. On March 11, 1904, Mrs. Frances Sherman, a retired Methodist missionary to Korea, started a mission school in Los Angeles with the help of the Woman's Home Mission Society of the Methodist Episcopal Church, South. Her primary purpose was to teach the Bible and English to Korean immigrants. The class was conducted every weekday evening, on Sunday the worship service was held at the same place. Later, Shin Heung-wu, mentioned earlier, served as a local pastor until his return to Korea in 1910 after earning his doctorate. Due to the absence of a pastor, for a while the congregation was merged with a Presbyterian church. On October 16, 1930, however, it became separate and independent again. The Reverend Hwang Sa-yong became pastor of what is today known as the Robertson Korean United Methodist Church, later led by such pastors as the Reverend Choe Yung-yong (Young Yong Choi) and the Reverend Pak Dae-hi (Dae Hee Park). Today it is the flagship church of the Korean Methodist Church on the West Coast. This church did not own its own building until 1944; on October 7, 1945, it was dedicated by a 150-member congregation.[19]

The Los Angeles church also tried to shoulder educational or political burdens for Korean immigrants. It taught English to Korean immigrants. It also helped to further the Korean independence movement by providing an interpreter at the trial of Korean patriots in San Francisco in 1908. In September 1924 supporters of Syngman Rhee (then provisional president of the Republic of Korea, headquartered in Shanghai, China) organized the Korean Residents' Society (*hanin kyomin hoe*) in Los Angeles, to oppose An Chung-ho's Great Korean National Association (*daehanin kukmin hoe*), which was established in 1909, and his Talent Cultivation Society. In 1928, to oppose An's Korean independence movement in Los Angeles, Rhee went there in person to integrate the Korean Residents' Society into the Comrade Society (*dongji hoe*) that he had established in Honolulu in 1921. In 1943, to advance his own political cause, he designated Los Angeles as the headquarters of the Comrade Society in North America. On April 11, 1943, he also issued his newspaper, the *North American Journal* (*pukmi shibo*), to compete with the *New Korea* (*shinhan minbo*), established by An Chung-ho in 1905 and still being published as a weekly in Los Angeles. Both papers advanced the cause of Korean independence.

We do not know for sure to what extent or in what way Korean Methodists were involved in the An-Rhee power strife. The number of Koreans in Los Angeles was extremely small, roughly forty to fifty, and there was no denominational consciousness, either Methodist or Presbyterian,[20] and no understanding of the value of separating church and state, so practically everyone was involved in all activities in the city, religious and political.

Chicago

A significant number of Koreans lived in Chicago during this period. Their first church, the Chicago Korean Methodist Church, came into being after the March 1919 Korean uprising against Japanese rule, in direct response to the spirit of the March First Independence Movement of 1919 in Korea. From the time of the annexation of Korea by Japan in 1910, Koreans had resisted the Japanese peacefully. On March 1, 1919, the Korean people abruptly but peacefully demanded immediate political independence in accordance with President Wilson's fourteen principles of self-determination adopted at Versailles in early 1919. This demand was rejected outright by the Japanese. Worse yet, a bloodbath followed.

In the midst of this crisis in Korea, the Chicago church was born. Kwak Yim-dae, a follower of An Chang-ho, conducted the first worship service to celebrate the Korean Independence Movement. After a three-year suspension, the worship service resumed in March 1922 at a rooming house located at Lake Park Avenue. On July 27, 1924, the Home Missionary Society of the Northern Illinois Conference established a Korean congregation in an American Methodist church basement located on Lincoln Avenue. The Reverend Kim Chang-jun was invited to be the pastor. He had been one of the thirty-three signatories of the Declaration of Korean Independence of March 1, 1919 (along with ten Methodists, both clergy and laity). After serving a short prison term in Korea, he came to the United States to work for the Chicago church.[21] Most of his church members were students associated with various institutions of higher learning in and around Chicago. Since church members were not great in numbers, they were a tightly knit group. Their life centered around the church, and again, there was little separation of religion and politics in their minds.

The Chicago church grew financially. In 1933 it acquired a $50,000 building at West Erie Street, later dedicated by Bishop Charles W. Brashares. Church membership reached nearly fifty. With potential growth in sight, the American Methodist mission helped the Korean church financially.[22] This church subsequently became the First Korean Methodist Church of Chicago. The Reverend Cha Hyun-hoe in particular should be noted for his important contributions to the Korean community as pastor of this flagship church in the Midwest.

New York

The New York Korean (Methodist) Church also deserves attention. In the wake of the 1919 Independence Movement, Koreans in New York, as elsewhere, established their own church. On April 18, 1921, the Reverend Kim Chong-sun, a Presbyterian pastor, became the first pastor of the New York Korean Church, but he returned to Korea a year later. As a result, on February 10, 1923, the church was merged with the Korean Methodist church. On April 23 it acquired an $18,000 church building located at West 2nd Street. In October 1927 it bought a $45,000 building at West 115th Street. This church was the only Korean church on the Eastern Seaboard. It has transcended denominational lines to this day and now calls itself the New York Korean Church. It is currently being pastored by the Reverend Choe Hyo-sop.[23]

New York attracted students, travelers, merchants, and officials. Therefore, the New York Korean Church primarily catered to their needs. Since the congregation was largely composed of transient residents, its membership was always small. As a result, the church always struggled for survival, financially and otherwise. In times of financial crisis, American Methodists always helped the Korean congregation in New York, as they had done elsewhere.

The New York church prospered in time. Its accomplishments have been impressive; it has produced outstanding leaders in the fields of government, business, religion, art, and education in Korea. The big names are so numerous that they cannot be listed here. Many former members of this church served as cabinet ministers for the most famous Korean Methodist, Syngman Rhee. Rhee once made a courtesy visit to this church when he became president of Korea.[24] As shown in this historic event, the New York church has epitomized Koreans' preference to maintain a close relationship between church and state.

The following are characteristics of Korean Methodist churches in the United States before 1945. First, many churches had to help members cope with their harsh lives. The early Korean immigrants were hopeless and helpless, spiritually and economically. To alleviate their problems, they first sought out the meaning of life on earth as well as in heaven. They found a haven in the church, however temporary it might be. Through their church life, they felt the warmth of their compatriots, and they communicated with one another in their mother tongue. Second, the churches provided immigrants with basic educational skills for survival and to improve their quality of life in an alien land. Third, the churches raised the level of political consciousness on the part of the Korean people, particularly after the Japanese annexation of Korea in 1910. Korean Christians in America, having been relatively well educated as compared to their compatriots in Korea, played an important role in dealing with the critical issues of the time, political, economic, spiritual, or otherwise. Fourth, the churches relied on the assistance of the Methodist Board of Mission and Home Mission for help in establishing themselves. Without material and moral help from American Methodists, in many cases Korean congregations could not have survived. At times physical survival was more important than spiritual salvation for Koreans. Their physical survival was made possible because the Methodist Episcopal Church had been committed to foreign-language congregations since 1819. A ban on Asian immigration (except for Filipinos) in 1905 and the subsequent total ban in 1924 forced the American Methodist church to actively work for the survival of various ethnic groups. The Korean Methodists survived without new immigrants from Korea.

THE TRIUMPHANT PERIOD, 1945 TO 1987

Build houses and live in them; plant gardens and eat their produce. (Jeremiah 29:5 RSV)

The Koreans regained independence with the American victory over Japan in August 1945. But their dream did not come true; their country was divided in two, the northern half controlled by the Soviet Union and the southern half by the United States. North Koreans started a war against the south in June 1950, with Russian aid. South Koreans received massive American support for the war. When Communist China entered the war, the situation was stalemated. In July 1953 both sides signed a truce, ending a three-year war. Worth noting is the fact that in search of political, economic, and religious freedom, 3 million North Koreans fled to the south during the war.

In the meantime, the United States Congress passed the Walter-McCarren Act in 1950, which allowed Asians to come to this country as immigrants again and also allowed Asian-born immigrants to acquire U.S. citizenship for the first time. The subsequent Immigration and Naturalization Act of 1965 finally abolished the discriminatory quota system (the 1924 Exclusionary Immigration Act) based on race, religion, or place of origin. Until 1965 the Korean population in this country had been the smallest in numbers among major Asian groups. For example, in 1920 there were 111,000 Japanese, 62,000 Chinese, 5,600 Filipinos, and 1,200 Koreans. By 1965, however, their respective figures were further reduced because of naturalization or death; among the alien residents were 3,189 Japanese, 4,057 Chinese, 3,180 Filipinos, and 3,165 Koreans. But the historic immigration law of 1965 increased the Korean population in the United States after almost half a century of stagnation. Within a decade or so, a big change appeared in the distribution of ethnic minorities, as Koreans took full advantage of the new law. In 1974, for example, the United States received 4,860 Japanese (53 percent increase), 18,056 Chinese (345 percent), 32,857 Filipinos (95 percent), and 28,028 Koreans (1,194 percent). As of 1974 there were 217,147 Koreans living in the United States. Since then about 30,000 to 40,000 Korean immigrants have been coming annually. By 1985 their number reached 840,000, and by June 1986, as mentioned at the outset, it was over 1 million.[25] If the present trend continues, Koreans undoubtedly will become the largest ethnic minority group among all Asians.

As the number of Korean immigrants grew rapidly, so too did that of Korean churches. There were 20 Korean American churches in 1970 and 1,000 in 1980. As of 1987, however, there are more than 1,600 Korean American churches throughout the United States. Likewise, in 1970 there were only six Korean Methodist churches, but by 1987 there were over 250

(200 churches already organized and 50 still in the process). According to Jonah Chang's article, published in the July-August 1981 issue of *Circuit Rider*, Koreans enjoyed a 1,000 percent increase in the number of their churches and members.[26]

This rapid church growth needs some explanation. After the Korean War in 1950, 3 million North Koreans, mostly Christians, fled to the south in search of freedom. As a result, the number of Korean Christians in the south quickly grew. The uprooted refugees from the north undoubtedly contributed to the rapid growth of Christianity in South Korea. As of 1984, 20 percent of the Korean population was considered Christian (15 percent Protestants and 5 percent Catholics), that is, 10 million Christians of the 40 million Koreans in the south. This miracle was performed just after Protestantism was introduced in Korea only 100 years ago. This growth rate is phenomenal by any standard.

The growth rate among the Koreans in the United States is even more startling; 70 percent are believed to be affiliated with Christian churches. This means that the number of Korean Christians in America increased more than three times, as compared to their counterparts in Korea. This growth in America has been attributed to loneliness and frustration among Korean immigrants, due largely to job, language, and other adjustment problems in an alien land. When the pattern of Korean immigration in recent years is examined, we find a marked change in it. For example, in the period 1965 to 1975, professionals were a dominant group, but from 1976 on their families and relatives became a much larger group. For example, in 1976 58.4 percent (17,983) of Korean immigrants entered the United States through the sponsorship of professionals. This figure doubled in five years. For example, in the period October 1981 to September 1982, 30,160 Koreans came to this country through the same channel.[27] In view of this fact, the above analysis seems largely valid. As the church traditionally played the role of both community center and worship place, people usually expected the church to solve their problems, both secular and sacred. But the church will have to meet the demands of many different kinds of people in the future.

To meet their demands, Korean Methodists launched the Membership Doubling Movement in 1984 in commemoration of the centennial of the introduction of Methodism in Korea. To implement those goals, the Korean caucus had three resolutions passed unanimously at the 1984 General Conference in Baltimore: (1) increasing the overall membership of American Methodists to 20 million, (2) increasing tithing, and (3) establishing five hundred new Korean Methodist churches and increasing membership of Korean Methodists to 100,000 by the year 2000. Although Koreans failed to set up an independent missional structure for Korean American ministry within the general church, they managed to create the National Committee on Korean American Ministry, under the supervision of the General Board of Global Ministries, of which the Reverend Chong Chun-su (Choonsoo Chung) is in charge. As a first step, this committee met on July 14, 1986, in New York and agreed to create the Mission for Korean American Ministry in five jurisdictions. This mission was called the Korean Provisional Mission. Dr. Cha Pung-no (Poong Ro Cha) was appointed the first mission superintendent for the Eastern Seaboard as of July 1987. Four more mission superintendents were appointed by 1988. For this historic task, Korean Methodists had earlier organized the Movement of Strengthening and Developing Korean-American United Methodist Church in Los Angeles on May 27-29, 1986. In addition to the creation of 500 churches and 100,000 members within the next ten years, this meeting also decided to work to enforce bilingual education for the training of future pastors, develop new churches, and produce programs for church growth. To put them into effect, an ad hoc committee was also established to raise funds from existing local churches. The target amount was $120,000 annually; each and every Korean church was asked to contribute 1 percent of its annual budget, beginning in 1987. At the same time, on an individual level, the so-called 500 Club was organized to facilitate the fund-raising drive. According to the plan, an individual can become a member of the 500 Club if he or she pays $100 a year for the next five years to defray expenses for the establishment of 500 new churches in the next ten years. As of this writing, it is reported that already eight churches have been committed and raised $4,559, and 32 individuals raised $3,810, for a total of $8,369.[28]

Subsequently, the same resolutions were adopted at the meeting of the National Association of Korean American United Methodist Churches, held in Los Angeles in January 1987. This body was ready to shoulder this mission. It was first organized in Los Angeles in late spring of 1973. About forty people attended the first nationwide meeting. The late Song Chong-yul (Charles C. Song) was elected president and served until 1976. His main concern was how to establish connectionalism between the general church and the Korean Methodist churches. From then on, every two years, it held a national meeting to elect a slate of new officers and to set new agendas. Cha Hyun-hoe of Chicago succeeded as the second president of this organization in 1976 and served until 1978. His interest was in developing new churches across the country. In 1978 he was succeeded by Dr. Kim Hae-chong (Hae Jong Kim), who currently serves as district superintendent in New Jersey. He tried to strengthen connectional ties among the Korean Methodist churches. Mr. Yi Eung-kyun of Honolulu was elected president in 1980; he emphasized the importance of evangelism. Dr. Kim Sung-wuk (Paul Kim) of Columbus, Ohio, succeeded him in 1982; he tried to solve the problem of transfer or appointment for Korean pastors. The next president, Dr. Sun Yun-kyung (Peter Sun) of Washington, D.C., continued to work on this problem; he was instrumental in bringing the issue of Korean pastoral appointments to the church's attention, and he managed to have resolutions passed on the matter at the 1984 General Conference in Baltimore. The Reverend Pak Dae-hi of Los Angeles, as current president (since 1986), has been enthusiastic about implementing those resolutions during his tenure. To follow them up, the School of Theology at Claremont, in cooperation with the General Board of Higher Education, established a bilingual master of divinity program primarily to train Korean-speaking clergy, under the leadership of Dr. Kim Chan-hi (Chan Hie Kim).

Many people are optimistic about the ability of the National Association of Korean American Methodist Churches to meet its financial target because of the increasing prosperity of the Korean American community. According to a study conducted by the Korean Chamber of Commerce in the Los Angeles area in 1985, the average annual income of 1,593 randomly surveyed Korean families was $13,675 in 1978 and $27,044 in 1984, double the amount in six years. It was also much higher than the average Anglo-American income, which was $20,885 as of 1983.[29] In fact, many Korean United Methodist churches have become financially self-sufficient, although they received financial assistance from The United Methodist Church, especially in their beginning stages. Since self-support is possible in a few years, new church development is realistic on the part of The United Methodist Church. Korean Methodist churches are also giving in the form of apportionment more faithfully than ever in building the kingdom of God on earth.

This financial progress has a lot to do with the educational level of Korean immigrants. New York City has the second largest number of Korean immigrants in the United States (Los Angeles has the highest). A recent survey indicates that there are about 200,000 Korean immigrants in the New York City area. Queens alone (one of the five boroughs in the city) has 20,000 Koreans, among whom 53 percent are known to be senior and junior college graduates. According to the category of their profession, 17 percent of them are engaged in highly skilled jobs such as medicine, law, engineering, and college teaching; 36 percent are in business, mostly medium and small size; and 37 percent are unskilled physical laborers.[30] This means that 53 percent of the Koreans in Queens are engaged in some kind of profession rather than physical labor. This also means that a considerable number of Korean immigrants in New York received their higher education when they were in Korea.

Asian Americans in general are doing well educationally because of their respect for scholarship, a part of Confucian tradition. At the present time, their children are doing far better than their parents. For example, as of December 1987, 25 percent of the student body at the University of California at Berkeley are Asian American students, and similarly, 10 percent of the students at Harvard University and other Ivy League schools are Asians. Because of this trend, there is a movement to curb Asian student enrollment in those schools. One can readily understand this problem in view of the fact that Asian Americans comprise less than 2 percent of the total population of the United States.

Although data for Korean students are not available at the time of this writing, Korean students, including Korean Methodists, must have represented their fair share among these college students. According to one study, however, 80 percent of high school graduates of Korean ancestry go to college, compared to 50 percent of Anglo students. Thus the economic status of the Koreans in Los Angeles and New York is not surprising, nor is it surprising to see Korean immigrants realize their dream for education through their children.

When opportunities to move to the United States were presented in the late 1960s and early 1970s, Koreans, particularly those from the north, grabbed them. Their migration coincided with the start of political persecution in South Korea. The Syngman Rhee regime had come to an end in 1960 because of student protests; when General Park Chung Hee introduced military dictatorship in 1961, the shaky democratic regime of President Yun Bo Sun collapsed. There has been no political freedom in South Korea since then.

Koreans who emigrated to the United States during these years scattered themselves everywhere, from Maine to Hawaii and from Alaska to Florida. Many, like their predecessors, settled in the major urban areas of Honolulu, Los Angeles, San Francisco, Chicago, and New York. Large numbers also settled in such cities as Seattle, Houston, Atlanta, Miami, and Washington, D.C. They are determined to stay anywhere there is an opportunity for a good life. In this respect Korean immigrants are different from other Asian minorities, who are concentrated mostly, if not exclusively, on the West Coast and Hawaii.

Once settled in their new home, Koreans started a series of political movements for the restoration of democracy and human rights in Korea. As in the past, Korean Methodists played a big role in these movements. Two such activists were Dr. Ham Sung-kuk (Michael Hahm) and Dr. Son Myong-kol (Myong Gul Son), both active leaders and members of the Association for Christian Korean Scholars in North America, a study group for the promotion of democracy and human rights in Korea. A substantial number of other Korean Methodists, both clergy and laity, were also concerned about the same issues.

Many of them morally and often politically as well supported Kim Dae Jung, a leader in opposition to the military regimes of both Park Chung Hee and Chun Doo Hwan in Korea. When in Washington as a political refugee from 1982 to 1985, Kim Dae Jung was frequently invited to Methodist churches to speak out on the issues of democracy and human rights in Korea. He was also granted an honorary doctorate for his contribution to Korean democracy by Emory University, a Methodist institution of higher learning in Atlanta. His wife, Yi Hi-ho, a Methodist, was equally well received; she was given an outstanding alumnus award at Scarritt College, a Methodist college for Christian workers in Nashville.

In sharp contrast, the Koreans in America did little or nothing about American politics more relevant to their livelihoods. One critic has said that Koreans, Christian and non-Christian alike, are not interested in protesting the high rent for business property in New York in any organized fashion, nor are they enthusiastic about supporting any local or national political candidates who promise to improve their plight. There are about 200,000 Koreans in New York, but among them only 23,000 are members of the Association for Korean Americans.[31] They do not get involved in American politics partially because of a lack of communication skills in English, a problem that had impeded their ancestors in Hawaii earlier. There is room for improvement in this regard if Korean Americans are to better their future in American society.

Korean Methodists did well in their involvements in the church; many moved into positions in the Methodist bureaucracy within a decade or so. Dr. Kim Chan-hi, formerly director of the Center for Asian American Ministries and currently professor of New Testament and Korean studies at Claremont School of Theology, began his career as the first Korean at the Board of Evangelism (now Board of Discipleship) in 1968. In 1976 another Korean, Dr. Son Myong-kol, was employed by the Board of Global Ministries. As of 1987 there are nine working for the national boards and agencies: four for Global Ministries, three for Discipleship, one for Communication, and one for Church and Society. In addition, three Koreans are serving as district superintendents: Dr. Kim Hae-chong in New Jersey, the Reverend Pak Chin-sung (Jeen Shoung Park) in California, and Dr. Cho Yong-chun (Young Joon Cho) in New York.

CONCLUSIONS

Korean Methodists in the United States have come a long way. Their humble start as sugar plantation workers in turn-of-the-century Hawaii was not propitious. For these early immigrants, America was not the land of plenty or opportunity; they did not achieve what they had intended religiously, economically, or politically. Until the 1950s, they suffered trials and tribulations and struggled for survival. Only in the years of the 1960s to the 1980s, when Koreans were given a second chance to come to this country, did they thrive. Unlike earlier immigrants who had only survived, the new immigrants succeeded economically and educationally (if not politically) due to their good education.

As directed by the God of Abram, Korean Methodists came to the new, promised land. As strange sojourners they first suffered in sugar fields in Hawaii, just as the Israeli people had suffered in the Sinai wilderness. As the Bible says, God has not failed his people. The present triumphant life of Koreans in California and New York is a shining example of God's grace. Koreans have already paid a dear price for their blessing through the blood and sweat of their ancestors in Hawaii.

The tasks remaining before us involve helping local Korean churches become a vital force within the general Methodist Church, maintaining close relations with the general church through the system of connectionalism, and maintaining Korean ethnic identity for second- and third-generation Korean Americans to come. Korean Americans need to take a more active part in the national church, for the betterment of all Christians.

NOTES

1. *hankuk shinbo* [*The Korea News*], Feb. 26, 1987, p. 4.

2. Ibid.

3. *donga ilbo* [*The East Asia Daily*], Feb. 12, 1987, p. 4; Yu Hong-yol, *History of Roman Catholicism in Korea* (Seoul, 1962), pp. 49-56. Yu says that some Korean Christians returned home from Japan.

4. Yi Yong-hon, *hankuk kidokkyo sa* [*A History of Christianity in Korea*] (Seoul: Concordia Press, 1985), pp. 19-20, 24-29.

5. Ibid., p. 26.

6. Ibid., p. 46.

7. Ibid., p. 59.

8. Ibid., p. 75-82.

9. Andrew W. Lind, *Hawaii's People* (Honolulu: University Press of Hawaii, 1955), p. 72; Yi Song-sam, *hankuk kamni kyohoe sa* [*The History of Korean Methodist Church*] (Seoul: General Board of Education of the Methodist Church, 1980), p. 357.

10. Ibid.; Ella Chun, "Korean Golden Jubilee," *Honolulu Advertiser*, Nov. 7, 1953.

11. Ibid., p. 358; Warren Y. Kim, *jaemi hanin oshipnyon sa* [*A 50-Year History of the Korean People in America*] (Reedley, Calif.: Charles Ho Kim Printing Co., 1959), pp. 47-50.

12. Ibid.

13. Ibid.

14. Kim, *jaemi hanin oshipnyon*, p. 28.

15. Ibid., pp. 47-50; Bong-youn Choy, *Koreans in America* (Chicago: Nelson-Hall, 1979), p. 95.

16. Ibid., pp. 85-86, 198-99.

17. Yi Song-sam, *hankuk kamni kyohoe sa*, p. 360; Kim, *jaemi hanin oshipnyon*, pp. 57-58, 317-31.

18. Yi Song-sam, *hankuk kamni kyohoe sa*, p. 360; Kim, *jaemi hanin oshipnyon*, pp. 58, 175.

19. Kim, *jaemi hanin oshipnyon*, pp. 63-65.

20. Ibid., pp. 42-43.

21. Yi Song-sam, *hankuk kamni kyohoe sa*, p. 362.

22. Ibid.; Kim, *jaemi hanin oshipnyon*, pp. 62-63.

23. Yi Song-sam, *hankuk kamni kyohoe sa*, p. 363; Kim, *jaemi hanin oshipnyon*, pp. 61-62; New York Korean Church, *New York hanin kyohoe yukshimnyon sa, 1921–1981* [*A 60-Year History of New*

York Korean Church, 1921–1981] (New York: New York Korean Church and Institute, 1981).

24. Ibid.

25. Eun Chol Cho (ed.), *A Survey Project for the Korean Mission Strategy in Northern Illinois Conference* (Chicago: The Korean United Methodist Church Association of Chicago and the Korean Methodist Clergy Fellowship of Chicago, 1985), p. 1.

26. Eun, *A Survey Project*, p. 2.

27. Ibid.

28. *yonhap kamnikyo soshik* [*The United Methodist News*] 4, no. 22 (Jan. 1987): pp. 3-4.

29. *honkook shinbo* [*The Korean News*], Feb. 26, 1987, p. 5.

30. *miju donga* [*The East Asia (Daily) in America*], Feb. 26, 1987, p. 1.

31. Ibid.

C H A P T E R   4

STRANGERS CALLED TO MISSION:

History of Chinese American United Methodist Churches

Wilbur W. Y. Choy

The Chinese were the first group of Asians who came in large numbers to the United States. Understandably, they came to the Pacific Coast, for this part of the country was the closest to China; the Pacific Ocean washes on the shores of both countries. The Chinese came about the time of the Gold Rush, around 1849. The gold fever bit them as it did other peoples on this and on other continents.

Furthermore, their labor was needed—in the homes, fields, mines, forests, railroad right-of-ways, and later on the railroads themselves. Their smaller stature and their physical agility made them especially desirable for work in the rugged and hazardous mountain passes during the building of the transcontinental railroads. So they came. By 1850 there were a sizeable number of them in California.

This was also the period when the missionary movement was gaining momentum. China, being a populous nation with an ancient civilization, was seen as one of the important fields for evangelization and missionary endeavor. The gospel of Jesus Christ must be preached and the love of God be made known to these people, that they may accept Christ and be saved. The same

I would like to thank the many local pastors who either provided interviews or have sent me written accounts of Chinese churches, and especially Dr. Edwar Lee, who provided a long interview and also made accessible documents in his possession. I am also grateful to the following institutions and their administrations for the courtesy extended me in permitting the use of their facilities: the Methodist Archives at University of the Pacific, the Pacific School of Religion, the School of Theology at Claremont, the University of Puget Sound, and the School of Theology at Claremont and at Lake Junaluska prior to its move to Drew University. Finally, I must apologize for any omissions or oversights. My prayer is that others will take up pen and do a more thorough piece of work.

interest and motivation prompted Chinese converts in America to be concerned about mission to the people back home in the old country.

This chapter will give a brief history of Methodist work among the Chinese in America. By Methodist, I am referring to The United Methodist Church and its antecedents, the Methodist Church and the Methodist Episcopal Church. The Methodist Episcopal Church, South; the Methodist Protestant Church; the Evangelical Church, and the United Brethren Church did not have work among the Chinese, although some of the local churches of these denominations did participate and helped with volunteers and funds in the work of Chinese missions in their communities.

In general, the history will be given in chronological order: The first section will record the first efforts of ministry among the Chinese immigrants, headed by Dr. and Mrs. Otis Gibson in the nineteenth century. The second section will look at the special work the Gibsons and others did among Chinese women. The third section will record efforts of the Chinese Missionary Society, which was a response originating among the Chinese Christians themselves. The fourth section will trace the process by which the Chinese churches became integrated into the geographical Annual Conferences during the middle of the twentieth century. The fifth section will look at each of the churches that were part of the Oriental Provisional Conference in 1952 and record each one's history briefly up to the present. The sixth section will touch on the new churches that began in the 1960s among the new immigrants, many of whom were refugees from Communist China; others were ethnic Chinese from various parts of Asia. This latter section is rather sketchy; some future writer will need to do more up-to-date and adequate research into this period.

THE CHINESE MISSION

The year was 1866. The city was Sacramento, California, near the place where gold was discovered. Three women of the Sixth Street Methodist Episcopal Church started a class for the Chinese of that city. The class was for both learning English and studying the Bible—the discovery of another kind of treasure.

The following year, the California Conference of the denomination, after several years' effort, was able to launch a mission to the Chinese. The Conference had been discussing the possibility of missional and evangelistic work among the Chinese immigrants, and a committee had been appointed to study the matter. One of the obstacles was the lack of available personnel who had an understanding of the Chinese. Literature was not a problem; during this period, Bibles and tracts in the Chinese language had been acquired from missionaries in China. But attempts to distribute this literature made little headway without trained personnel.[1] Now there was the possibility of such trained leadership, in the persons of Dr. and Mrs. Otis Gibson, missionaries in Fukien, China, who had had to return to this country because of Mrs. Gibson's health. The Board of Missions agreed to send this couple to San Francisco.

Dr. Gibson started by looking over what work was being done by other churches among the Chinese at that time. Among the several Protestant groups, the Presbyterians seemed to be making some progress. As for local Methodist efforts, the Chinese Sabbath school started by the Methodist women in Sacramento seemed to be the most effective. As a result, he decided to use the Sacramento school as a model for efforts elsewhere. He did so in the belief that "these schools will be the means of introducing the Chinese to our best citizens, of acquainting them with the spirit and genius of our institutions, and leading them gradually to adopt our higher form of civilization and our purer faith."[2]

Within a year, Dr. Gibson had established similar schools in San Francisco, Stockton, Marysville, Santa Cruz, and San Jose, along with the one in Sacramento. The work continued to expand. Schools were started in Oakland, Berkeley, Watsonville, Los Angeles, and Pasadena. In addition to these points in California, work was also begun in Salem and Portland in the state of Oregon and Seattle, Tacoma, and Port Townsend in Washington. All this was done in ten years.

It should be noted that in every case of these schools and missions, the work was started and carried out by Women's Home Missionary Societies and other volunteers. There was usually a local committee or board of managers. These groups often continued to be a support group even after the mission became organized as churches with Chinese pastors.

Skepticism and Apathy

Soon after starting his work in San Francisco, Dr. Gibson launched into a fund-raising campaign for the purpose of building a mission house in that city. His efforts took him to many parts of the country, where he spoke and preached. Sometimes he met with skepticism and apathy, for there were those who wondered about making these "strangers" too welcome, or who questioned whether the gospel was really for these heathen people. However, there were others who did respond. These latter saw the situation as truly a call to mission by God for that period of time. After much effort and prayer on his part and help from the general church, Dr. Gibson saw his dream come true. The mission house was built. It was dedicated on Christmas Day, 1870.[3]

In addition to the mission house, which included a chapel and classrooms, there was also a "storefront" gospel hall located on Jackson Street, more in the heart of Chinatown. The mission house was in what was a residential area, at the time. As a matter of fact, the adjacent property later acquired was the residence of a ship captain.

Revival meetings were held at the gospel hall. It was also the place for Chinese preachers to begin their ministry. The first such preacher was the Reverend Sing Mi Hu, who was ordained a deacon in the Foochow Conference in China. Unfortunately, the Chinese in San Francisco were almost entirely Cantonese speaking. Hu spoke the Foochow dialect, as did Dr. Gibson. Although he tried to learn Cantonese, Hu found it difficult and became discouraged. After two years, he decided to return to Foochow.

By this time, the first baptized Chinese at the Methodist Mission began to assist Dr. Gibson. His name was Loke Chee Chow. After Hu returned to China, Chow became the assistant preacher to Dr. Gibson. He was the first Chinese in America to be given a Methodist exhorter's license and subsequently a local preacher's license. He did not go on to become an ordained minister, however.

With schools and missions located in the states of Washington, Oregon, and California, just trying to keep in touch with them was an overwhelming undertaking. Dr. Gibson needed help. In 1878 the Board of Missions sent A. J. Hanson to assist Gibson. After working several years with Dr. Gibson in San Francisco and other points in California, Hanson was appointed to Portland, Oregon. It was also decided to make the Chinese work in the states of Washington and Oregon a separate mission from the one in California. Dr. Hanson became the superintendent of the Chinese Mission in the Pacific Northwest in 1882.

Dr. Gibson continued his work as superintendent of the Chinese Mission in California, with its many stations, until ill health necessitated his leaving the work. In 1885 Frederick J. Masters, who had been a British Methodist missionary in Canton, was appointed to succeed Dr. Gibson.

In the seventeen years that Dr. Gibson was the superintendent of the Chinese Mission, he worked indefatigably for the Lord and for the Chinese people. He started schools and missions. He established a women's home that later became the Gum Moon Home. He spoke on behalf of the Chinese Mission in many parts of the country and raised funds for its support. He fought against anti-Chinese forces in San Francisco, in the state of California, and before congressional committees, as he and other Protestant leaders testified against anti-Chinese legislation. He appeared in court in defense of Chinese women who were violated in their person and in their human rights.[4] At one point, anti-Chinese mobs burned Gibson in effigy. As the Reverend Hon Fan Chan wrote in his "History of Chinese Methodism on the Pacific Coast," "Dr. Gibson . . . suffered much as the champion of the Chinese cause. He was misjudged by the church, the government, and the public at large."[5]

Dr. Gibson was not only the founder of the Chinese Methodist Mission but also the founder of the Japanese Methodist Mission. Ten years after he began work among the Chinese in San Francisco, he started classes for Japanese immigrants and invited them to the mission house in Chinatown.[6]

Frederick Masters carried on the work of the mission diligently and energetically. As his predecessor had done, he defended the Chinese against discrimination. As a linguist and a scholar who spoke the Cantonese dialect well, he was liked and respected in the Chinese community.

It was during Dr. Master's ministry at the mission that a number of Chinese converts responded to the call to preach. One of these was Hon Fan Chan. Chan had been a student in a Wesleyan mission school in Canton, China. In 1890 Chan came to San Francisco and brought with him a letter of introduction. Dr. Masters employed him as an assistant at the gospel hall, and Chan did some of the preaching there. Because of his youth, he became known in San Francisco as the "Boy Preacher." He was apparently a powerful and engaging speaker. Dr. Edwar Lee, who was a youth in the San Francisco Chinese Church when Chan was pastor, remembered that Chan preached to overflowing crowds and that often people of the other Chinatown churches and of no Church Affiliation came, as well as the Methodists.

By 1893 there were in the California Conference of the Methodist Episcopal Church language ministries to the German-speaking, the Scandinavian-speaking, the Japanese-speaking, and the Chinese-speaking peoples. Each group of the churches had been missions under the Conference. By the latter part of the century, however, the Conference thinking was that these missions should be organized as districts in the Conference. Thus the Chinese Mission became the Chinese District, with Dr. Frederick J. Masters as presiding elder. In those days, the term "district superintendent" was not yet in use. As mission superintendent and presiding elder, Dr. Masters served the Chinese churches for nearly fifteen years.

Then came the following superintendents: F. D. Bovard (1899 to 1900) and J. D. Hammond (1900 to 1903). It was during Hammond's ministry that the site which is now the Chinese United Methodist Church was purchased. Others were H. B. Heacock (1903 to 1905), Thomas Filben (1905 to 1906), Edward James (1906 to 1914), W. C. Evans (1914 to 1915), George L. Pearson (1915 to 1922), John Hedley (1922 to 1925), D. H. Klinefelter (1925 to 1927), and John Wilson (1927 to 1934).

H. B. Heacock had become acquainted with the Chinese Mission because at one point he was the presiding elder of the San Francisco district during part of Dr. Gibson's term of service. While Dr. Heacock was superintendent, there was a change of structure again. The Chinese churches were organized as a Mission Conference. Bishop Luther B. Wilson presided at its organizational meeting.[7]

During Dr. James' term the 1906 earthquake hit San Francisco. Much of the city was destroyed by fire, including the mission house. In the manner of Dr. Gibson, Dr. James traveled all over, speaking and raising funds for the restoration of the mission and the construction of a new mission house. His efforts and the responses from many people, with grants from the national church, made it possible to construct new facilities. However, the congregation also had to be rebuilt, for the earthquake and its resulting devastation had scattered the members and constituents. As a concerned pastor, he searched out his flock. New people were brought in as well. The school program likewise was reinstituted.

In 1908, during Dr. James' term as superintendent, the Chinese Mission in California adopted the name Pacific Chinese Mission. It was in 1914 when W. C. Evans was superintendent that the work in the Pacific Northwest was reunited with that of the churches in California. A fatal illness ended Evans' term prematurely.

George L. Pearson became the next superintendent, and he served eight years. During his tenure, the Mexicali Church became a part of the mission.

In the 1920s, following Pearson, John Hedley, D. H. Klinefelter, and John Wilson succeeded to the superintendency of the mission, with Dr. Wilson serving the longest term, from 1927 to 1934 when he retired. One of the things that these men had in common was that they had served as missionaries in China.

By 1924 Chinese immigration had come to a virtual halt because of the Chinese Exclusion Act. Other discriminatory legislation affecting the Chinese-American community denied aliens the right to own land or real estate and forbade them to become naturalized as citizens.

This was also the time, following World War I, when there was a decade of economic well-being followed by the crash of Wall Street and the Great Depression. With the Depression, many Chinese returned to China. These conditions along with other sociological and economic reasons meant that some of the cities and towns where there had been Chinese communities saw those communities decline. Some of the churches closed.

After Dr. Wilson's retirement, the Chinese churches of the mission came under the supervision of the presiding elders/district superintendents of their districts. Dr. Walter Torbet, field secretary of the Board of Missions, served as coordinator. This continued until 1939, when the three branches of Methodism—Methodist Episcopal, Methodist Episcopal South, and Methodist Protestant Churches—united. With that union, Chinese, Filipino, and Korean churches on the Pacific Coast were brought together to form the California Oriental Mission.[8]

WORK AMONG WOMEN

The immigration of Chinese to the United States was motivated partly by the need for cheap labor in the developing West and partly by the hope of striking gold on the part of the Chinese themselves. Thus it was that the name for the strait into San Francisco Bay, the Golden Gate, had several meanings. For many Chinese, it meant the gate to the gold fields. In the first century of their migration to this country, the common Chinese term for the United States was the "Golden Mountain." Gradually, this became the designation for San Francisco primarily. The agency fulfilling our church's mission working with women in San Francisco's Chinatown is named Gum Moon, the Chinese term for Golden Gate—the gateway to new opportunities, a new life!

Since the early Chinese immigrants came to build railroads, to do farm labor, and to mine gold, they were primarily males. A few women did come later, but they were the wives and daughters of the few merchants who came to do business here. Other women who came were imported as domestics or for the slavery of prostitution. The latter group represented the largest numbers.

From the very beginning of his service as superintendent of the Chinese Mission in San Francisco, Otis Gibson recognized the need to do something intentionally for Chinese women. As he said, "To neglect the women in the ministrations of the Gospel to the Chinese would only tend to strengthen them in their heathen ideas that women have no souls and no personal rights in themselves, outside of the will of their parents, husbands, or masters. Something must be done."[9]

Despite his old-fashioned way of putting things, his recognition of the rights of women as children of God is unmistakable and passionate, as well as compassionate.

"Something must be done" for the Chinese women, but Gibson did not know what. Neither did anyone else. About this time, a few prostitutes escaped from their masters. A Mr. Loomis of the Presbyterian mission helped them find asylum in a home operated by the San Francisco Ladies' Protective and Relief Society. Then, a concerned church woman was able to visit some Chinese women in their rooms and tenements and reported that there were probably many other Chinese women trapped in this kind of slavery who would escape if they could find refuge somewhere.

This convinced Gibson that along with the mission house's facilities for evangelization and education, which were geared for men, there needed to be a "Female Department," a refuge or shelter for women escaping this kind of degradation. When the mission house was built, the third floor of the building was planned as the "Female Department." It was not until a year later, however, that it was actually used for the designated purpose.

On October 20, 1871, Dr. Gibson received a note from a police captain of the San Francisco police department. It told of a Chinese woman who had been rescued from drowning in San Francisco Bay by a black man who had been fishing out there. Dr. Gibson went to the police station to see the woman. She told him that she wanted to go to the mission, but she did not want to go "to Jackson Street," obviously the location of the brothel where she had been. The woman's name was Jin Ho. After staying at the mission house for a year,

Jin Ho went to work in a Christian home. Later she married a Chinese man.

Other Chinese women who were in similar circumstances heard of Jin Ho's experience. Some of them escaped from the brothels and sought refuge at the mission house also. It became necessary to have "a lady missionary whose whole time should be devoted to teaching and developing in every way these poor waifs."[10] Miss Laura Templeton of Sacramento was selected. In her report of 1874, Miss Templeton reported that fourteen women and girls were in the "Asylum."[11] By this time, this facility was serving not only as a shelter for women but also as a home for orphans.

From the beginning of his work in Chinatown, Dr. Gibson had appealed to the women of the Methodist churches in San Francisco to help, especially with the work among the Chinese women. Eleven women responded, and on October 20, 1870, the Women's Mission Society of the Pacific Coast was formed. It provided help and support to the work, both financially and with volunteer workers.

After the 1906 earthquake and fire destroyed the original building, the society, through the efforts of its members up and down the Pacific Coast, helped to raise the funds for constructing a new home separate from the mission house. Additional property adjacent to the mission house was purchased. A woman architect named Julia Morgan did the designing, and the new home was built. It was dedicated on January 27, 1912.[12] This is the building of Gum Moon Home today.

During the period following the earthquake to the time the new building was ready for occupancy, the home carried on in temporary quarters in Berkeley, across the Bay from San Francisco. Telling about the day of the earthquake and the subsequent events, Carrie Davis, who was superintendent of the home at that time and who had served a total of ten years, wrote in her journal that it was "a day never to be forgotten."

> Amidst the crashing of chimneys and cracking and tearing of the walls and everything movable falling around us we all escaped from the building without a scratch. (This was 5 A.M.) Without food, but for a few crackers and oranges, we watched the fire devouring block after block. . . . By daylight we heard that all the mission houses were gone and all that part of the city.
>
> At 7 A.M. we started on our march to the Ferry to try and get across the Bay if possible. . . . At 4 P.M. we reached the Ferry and it was with thankful hearts we sank on a seat on the boat.[13]

Eventually, the operation of this work among women became part of the Women's Division of the general church. By 1940, at the time of the unification of the Methodist Church, the needs in the Chinese community had changed. The decision was made to turn Gum Moon Home into a residence hall "for employed and student Chinese girls."[14]

At the time of this writing, Gum Moon has residents from eight different countries. The women range in age from seventeen to seventy years of age. The executive director is Angela Chang, the first administrator of Gum Moon who is of Chinese ancestry. In addition to providing a residence for women in transition, Gum Moon offers a program called Asian Women's Resources Center. This center provides Asian women of the community as well as residents with classes in English, typing, and other skills in the job development area.

CHINESE MISSIONARY SOCIETY

After decades of working within the structure of the Methodist Episcopal Church, the Chinese members of the mission, lay and clergy, felt a call to do their own missional and evangelism work in their homeland of Guangdong, China.[15]

In 1890 an effort was made to organize a missionary society, as some of the other Chinese Christians had done. By the turn of the century, the Chinese Methodists did indeed launch a Chinese Methodist missionary society. Its expressed purpose was to establish missions in the province of Guangdong and in the districts of that province.

By polity agreement among the several American denominations working in China, American Methodists did not work in that southern province, although the British Methodists did. The reasons why the Methodist Church of Great Britain had missions in southern China are at least two: Britain had a special relationship with Hong Kong, a city at the tip of Guangdong Province, and the polity agreements were primarily among the American denominations and their mission agencies. Since the Methodist Episcopal Church had agreed not to work in Guangdong and the Chinese Methodist churches in the United States had no direct relationship with the British missions, the Chinese Methodists in America decided to form the Chinese Missionary Society as a separate entity from the Pacific Chinese Mission, which was an official part of the Methodist Episcopal Church. The society was thus unofficial as far as the denomination or the California Conference was concerned. It was made up of Chinese pastors and lay representatives only. The white superintendent and the denomination's Board of Missions were not involved. The officers were Chinese. The programs and plans were designed and implemented by the Chinese themselves. The society was also an expression of freedom and independence. It was a movement for self-determination, self-support, and self-propagation, before the term "three self movement" was coined. It was an expression of the society's maturity in Christian discipleship.

In 1901 the Chinese Missionary Society commissioned its first missionary to China. His name was Kwai Yue. Yue was one of the first Chinese converts to respond to the call to the ordained ministry. He had been a student at the Methodist school in Oakland and became a Christian. Later, he took the Conference Course of Studies for Methodist preachers under Superintendent Frederick Masters. During this period he served the missions in Stockton and in Sacramento.

Because of health reasons, he thought he ought to return to China. He also felt that he ought to continue in the ministry. Thus he volunteered to go to China as a missionary on behalf of the Chinese Missionary Society. The society agreed and raised $2,000 for this missionary work. Chinese Methodists in Canton, some of whom were converted in the mission in this country, raised another $1,000 to help launch this enterprise.[16]

At this time Yue was only an ordained deacon.[17] It was not until 1905 that he qualified for the elder's order. He was elected to that order by the California Conference and was duly ordained by Bishop James Bashford, who was resident bishop in Shanghai, China. The bishop made a special trip to Canton for that purpose.[18] Yue remained in missionary service for fourteen years, helping to establish several congregations and schools in and around Canton.[19]

The churches in China that were started with the help of the Chinese Missionary Society in America never were a part of the Methodist Church in China. Later, when many of the Christian denominations in China united to form the Church of Christ in China, these churches became a part of that church.

As for the Chinese Missionary Society itself, it lost momentum even as the Chinese churches went into decline in the second and third decades of this century. Perhaps its last organized activity was to raise some money for its sister churches in China for post–World War II repairs to the buildings there. As a probationary member of the Conference, the author remembers participating in that effort.

MOVING TOWARD INTEGRATION

With the unification of the three branches of Methodism, there began a process of integration. This was not so much the integration of congregations, although some of that did come about later; today, many churches on the Pacific Coast are multi-ethnic. In this chapter, "integration" is used for the process by which separate groupings of churches, by language and ethnic background of members, gradually come together structurally and organizationally. This has also been referred to as "coming into the mainstream of the denomination."

In June 1939, at the San Francisco Chinese Methodist Episcopal Church, the last session of the Pacific Chinese Mission Conference was held.[20] Bishop

James Chamberlain Baker presided. It was also the first session of the California Oriental Mission Conference. Three branches of Methodism had united, and three different Asian groups were being brought together. Both the Northern and Southern Methodists had Korean churches. The Filipino churches had been missions of the Methodist Episcopal Church. Now these two were to join with the Chinese churches to form the Oriental Mission Conference. The Filipino churches were San Francisco, Oakland, Stockton, and Seattle, Washington. The Korean churches were San Francisco, Oakland, Los Angeles, and Delano. The Chinese churches were San Francisco, Oakland, Sacramento, Stockton, Los Angeles, Pasadena, and Mexicali, Mexico.

Dr. Ernest S. Lyons, a returned missionary to the Philippines, was appointed superintendent. One of his concerns was to develop more indigenous leadership among the Asians, who would assume more of the decision making. In consultation with Bishop Baker, Dr. Lyons worked for the mission to become a Provisional Annual Conference. In 1944 the General Conference passed an enabling act "permitting the Mission to organize as a Provisional Annual Conference when it shall have complied with the provisions of the Discipline."[21]

Bishop Baker was thoroughly in agreement with these developments. In 1943, as a matter of fact, he had appointed Edwar Lee as assistant superintendent. Dr. Lyons was at retirement age and needed help. It was also a step in preparing for the anticipated new status of the mission.

Thus in 1945 the California Oriental Mission took formal action to become a Provisional Annual Conference. Ministers who held their memberships in the California Annual Conference now transferred them to the new Provisional Annual Conference. Ministers in full connection were Key H. Chang, Amadeo Fayloga, Dionisio Gonzalo, Ha Tai Kim, Tark Kim, Edwar Lee, George Lowe, Ermie Obien, Tso-Tin Taam, and Wun-Bew Wong. Wilbur Choy was a probationer. Hiram Fong was a supply pastor. George H. Colliver had also been appointed to the mission, but his full-time appointment was to the faculty of the College of the Pacific in Stockton; thus he remained a member of the California Annual Conference, later to be known as the California-Nevada Conference.

The Reverend Edwar Lee was appointed the superintendent of the newly organized California Oriental Provisional Conference. He was the first Chinese American to fill such a position in the church. He was also the first American-born Chinese to answer the call to ministry in the Methodist Church. Lee was born in San Francisco and grew up in that city's Chinatown. He attended Chinese language schools there, as well as the public schools. Thus he spoke the Chinese language (Cantonese) fluently. His education beyond high school was received at the College of the Pacific, the University of California, and the Pacific School of Religion. He was subsequently honored by the College of the Pacific with a doctor of divinity degree.

Edwar Lee was one of the founders of the Chinese Christian Youth Conference, which met at Lake Tahoe Presbyterian conference grounds. It follows then that in his ministry as superintendent, he encouraged local churches in their educational and youth programs.

In 1945, the same year the Provisional Conference was established, World War II ended. Soon thereafter, new people were arriving from across the Pacific, and many of them were coming to our churches. The need for a Chinese language ministry was obvious. At the same time, a new generation of Chinese Americans had grown up, who were primarily English speaking. Bilingual services became the norm.

However, much more could have been done for that generation of Chinese Americans. Bilingual services helped. But perhaps the Japanese churches took the better step, one with more lasting benefits, when some of their churches inaugurated separate English services with American-born pastors. The educational and cultural orientation of the new generation of Chinese Americans was American. They were struggling to make their way socially, economically, and politically in an American society that was not always friendly. They needed pastors who could understand them better and could speak to their need. Chinese Methodist churches may well have lost an opportunity to serve many of that generation.

Another need of the Chinese churches was lifted up by Dr. Edwar Lee in his "State of the Conference" report of 1948:

> It has been my conviction that if we are to do an influential piece of work, we must have proper and adequate facilities in which to do it. Some of our plants not only do not reflect credit to the name of The Methodist Church, but are actually detrimental to the carry on of effective education and of Christian fellowship. It is toward remedying this situation that I have devoted a large share of my time and energy.[22]

During Dr. Lee's term of office, almost every one of our churches built or acquired new facilities. Among the Chinese churches, Oakland, Los Angeles, and Sacramento built new facilities. Stockton acquired new property. San Francisco remodeled its sanctuary.

In 1948 the General Conference of the Methodist Church adopted enabling legislation to integrate the several Provisional Conferences in the connection that were organized along ethnic lines. In particular, it was referring to the Latin-American Provisional Conference, Pacific Japanese Provisional Conference, and the California Oriental Provisional Conference, in the Western Jurisdiction.

76

By 1952 the California Oriental Provisional Conference became the first of the ethnic minority Conferences to integrate its churches with the geographical Annual Conferences. Thus the Chinese church and the Korean church, both of Los Angeles, became member churches of the Southern California-Arizona Conference. The Filipino church of Seattle became a part of the Pacific Northwest Conference. The remaining churches became members of the California-Nevada Conference: the Chinese churches of Oakland, Sacramento, San Francisco, and Stockton; the Filipino churches of Oakland, San Francisco, Stockton, and Vallejo; and the Korean churches of Delano, Oakland, and San Francisco.[23]

THE CHINESE CHURCHES
OF THE PROVISIONAL CONFERENCE

At this point a few words should be recorded about each of the Chinese churches and pastors in the Provisional Conference in 1952.[24]

Oakland

The Oakland Chinese church at the time of integration and merger was served by Edwar Lee. He had served it as associate pastor for four years. Then, in 1939, upon the retirement of the Reverend Lok Shang Chan, he was appointed pastor. Later, when he became the superintendent of the Provisional Conference, he continued as the pastor-in-charge. At various times, he had assistant pastors.

It was with his ministry that English became an important part of the worship service. A Chinese language school was conducted in the church for many years, but the need for such a school was being met by a large community school. Thus this program was phased out by the time of World War II. Evening English classes had also been one of the strong parts of this church's program, but by the late 1930s the demand for this program declined. However, by the 1950s there was again a large influx of new immigrants and refugees, and a new program of teaching English was started. This was part of the program coordinated by Miss Ruth Gress, who had been a missionary in Fukien, China.

By 1952 the Oakland Chinese church had built their new home. It was located on the same property in the heart of Oakland's Chinatown. The architecture was in the style of a Chinese palace, built for the King of Kings. A decade later, adjacent property was purchased and a social hall and additional rooms for the church school were constructed.

Dr. Edwar Lee retired in 1970 and was succeeded by the Reverend John Chow, who transferred in from the United Church of Christ of China in Hong

Kong. During Chow's ministry, a separate English service was established, with the Reverend John Chamberlain as associate pastor and English preacher.

Los Angeles

In 1952 the Chinese church in Los Angeles, which was within the bounds of the Southern California-Arizona Conference, became a part of that Conference with the integration process. In a sense, it was a returning home for the Los Angeles church, for in the early years of the Los Angeles Chinese Mission, it was a part of the Southern California Conference.

At the time of integration, the Reverend Wun-Bew Wong was the pastor. Wong had been a student at San Francisco Theological seminary. He came in 1940 as the Chinese-speaking assistant to Ernest Lyons, who was acting as pastor of the church as well as serving as superintendent for the Mission Conference. The Reverend Sing Kai Chan had retired in 1933 after serving the church for eight years. Others who served as pastors before Wong were Frank Fung and Lim P. Lee.

In the mid-1940s, the city of Los Angeles began an urban renewal program that included the relocating of Chinatown to a new site. Under Wong's leadership, a piece of property in this new area was purchased. Funds were raised, and a new sanctuary with educational facilities was constructed in traditional Chinese-style architecture. It was consecrated in 1948 by Bishop Baker. Less than two years later, the new resident bishop, Dr. Donald H. Tippett, dedicated the church. In that short time, the congregation was able to pay off the mortgage! For his outstanding leadership, Wong was honored with a doctor of divinity degree by California Western University of San Diego.

When Dr. Wong retired in 1970, he was succeeded by the Reverend Joseph Ma, who transferred from the United Church of Christ of San Diego. During Ma's ministry, many Chinese families were moving to Orange County, east of Los Angeles, including families of the Los Angeles Chinese church. Some of these families working with Ma helped to organize a new Chinese congregation in Orange County.

Ma retired in 1978, and the Reverend Leo Hsu became the pastor and continues to serve there. Hsu is from the Hong Kong Methodist Church. In 1984 the Reverend Miyeko Uriu, a Japanese American clergywoman, was appointed by Bishop Jack Tuell as associate pastor responsible for English worship services and youth work.

Sacramento

In 1952 the Reverend Hiram Fong, a local elder, was pastor of the Chinese Church of Sacramento. Fong was a businessman and banker who had completed studies as a supply pastor. By the time of integration, he had served the church in Sacramento for over twenty years. The Reverend George Lowe was associate pastor, responsible for youth programs and religious education and for preaching in English. Lowe was ordained in the United Church of Canada. In 1954 the Reverend Leo Fong transferred in from Arkansas after graduating from Perkins School of Theology to succeed Lowe.

For many years the church was located near downtown Sacramento. Many Chinese families lived in that area, for it was also near Chinatown. In the 1950s, the state of California, of which Sacramento is the capital city, began to acquire property near the church for state buildings. The city of Sacramento launched an urban renewal program about the same time. Thus the church sold its property and relocated to the southern part of the city, to which many of its members and constituents had moved. A new building was constructed with a sanctuary and classrooms for the Sunday school.

One of the great public services of Hiram Fong and the church was sponsoring a number of refugees of the Communist Revolution in China. They found employment and housing for these new people and provided them a ministry of support in many other ways.

In 1966 the church celebrated its one-hundredth anniversary. It had begun in 1866 as a Chinese Sabbath school led by three ladies of the Sixth Street Methodist Episcopal Church.

In 1968 Hiram Fong retired. The present pastor is Benjamin B. K. Chiu, who transferred in from the Singapore Methodist Church in 1980. Other pastors who served the church in the intervening years were Wilbur Choy, David Swope, Edwar Lee, Man-King Tso, and Calvin Wong.

San Francisco

The Reverend Tso Tin Taam was the pastor of this church at the time of integration. This church grew out of the first Chinese Mission of the Methodist Episcopal Church, established by Otis Gibson in 1868, and it occupies the same site as the old mission, though not the same building. Taam had been pastor since 1938. He came from Canton, China, where he had been on the faculty of the Union Theological College. He followed the Reverend David K. Lee, who served the church two years as an accepted supply pastor.

At that time the pastor of the Chinese church of San Francisco was also appointed to the faculty of the Hip Wo School, an interdenominational Chinese language school. It was originally a cooperative enterprise of the Baptist, Congregational, Presbyterian, and Methodist churches and their respective boards of mission. At different times, the Baptists and the Presbyterians withdrew. This meant that the school, which had been housed in a Presbyterian building, had to relocate. Under Taam's leadership, the Chinese Methodist Church opened its doors to the school and remodeled its building for the school's use.

After World War II, the church launched the Direct China Relief project, collecting clothing primarily but also food, medicine, and medical supplies for the relief of postwar China. The project continued until the Communist Revolution.

During his years as pastor of the San Francisco Chinese church, Taam was active in the Chinese community and was elected president of the Chinese Benevolent Association for several terms. He became known as "Mayor of Chinatown." The Pacific School of Religion conferred the doctor of divinity degree upon him in 1955.

In 1968 T. T., as he was affectionately known, retired and was succeeded by the Reverend Timothy Tam, who transferred from the United Church of Canada.

Stockton

In 1952 the Stockton Chinese church was known as the Chinese Christian Center. Dr. George H. Colliver, appointed to the Chinese Methodist Mission of Stockton in 1936, was responsible for the name change. With more than a hundred children and youth coming to the building throughout the week for a variety of activities, Chinese Christian Center seemed a more appropriate name.

Five years earlier, Lim P. Lee, a college student, assisted the Reverend Frank Fung with the boys' class in Sunday school. From the class, Lim organized a boys' club. Meanwhile, some of the women had started a girls' group; Dr. Dora Ames Lee, a physician, became one of its counselors. In 1932 Lim P. Lee was appointed the student pastor. Upon his graduation from college in 1934, two other students, Glenn Young and Harry Chin, took over the work for a year each. Then Dr. Walter Torbet, the field executive of the Board of Missions, approached Dr. Colliver to assume responsibility for this mission. Dr. Colliver was chairman of the department of Bible and religious education at the College of the Pacific. He had already become acquainted with the Mission through the previously mentioned student pastors, all of whom had studied with him.

Dr. Colliver accepted the appointment in addition to teaching at the college. Not only he, but Mrs. Colliver as well, provided the Chinese children and youth with a ministry that was most appreciated—warmth and concern from a Christian pastor and family that they had not had a chance to experience. It was Dr. Colliver's intention not only to provide a special ministry to the Chinese community with emphasis on the children and youth, but especially to develop indigenous leadership from within that community. Three young women, Jackie Ong, Beulah Ong Kwoh, and Daisy Toy Poon, in successive terms served as lay student preachers. Lois

Kanegawa Yee served a number of years as Girls' Work director. Her husband, Skipper Yee, served as Boys' Work director. During his twenty years' ministry among the Chinese Americans of Stockton, Colliver provided opportunity and inspiration for at least two generations of Chinese American youth of that community to develop leadership, to pursue a variety of professions with confidence and hope, and to do so in the faith that God in Christ was with them all the way.

Wilbur Choy, one of Dr. Colliver's students and a product of the Chinese Christian Center of Stockton, was appointed assistant pastor for the Stockton church in 1944. Upon graduation from seminary, he was appointed pastor in 1949. In 1956 the Chinese Christian Center merged with Clay Street Methodist Church to form St. Mark's Methodist Church, using the Clay Street location.

The Clay Street Methodist Church had a mixed congregation of several ethnic groups, with the majority being white. The newly merged congregation was even more visibly multi-ethnic, but it had a Chinese majority. The sanctuary was remodeled, and new furnishings added. An educational building with a gymnasium was built. Choy continued as pastor of the merged church until 1959.

Since then, other pastors have been Jun W. Jue, Charles Yue, James Bradford, Joseph Yong, and Leo Fong. Fong has been serving St. Mark's since 1979. Under his pastorate, the church has become even more diverse and multi-ethnic.

Mexicali

The Chinese Methodist Mission of Mexicali became a part of the Pacific Chinese Mission during the Reverend George Pearson's term as superintendent, from 1915 to 1922. It had always been served by a neighboring Methodist pastor, usually of Calexico just across the border. Other times, supply pastors or lay missionaries carried on the work. It remained a part of the California Oriental Mission after unification.

At various times the Mexicali Mission sponsored a Chinese language school and operated a dormitory for single men. From time to time, the Chinese pastors of the Los Angeles Chinese Mission would make a trip to Mexicali to conduct a series of meetings or to hold preaching services in the Chinese language.

By the 1940s, the government of Mexico had nationalized all church property; church facilities were then leased back to the worshiping congregations. With the organization of the Provisional Conference, the Mexicali Chinese Mission became a part of the Methodist Church of Mexico.

When this writer visited Mexicali in 1978, a few members of the Methodist

Church there were of Chinese ancestry. Classrooms formerly used by the Chinese language school were now used by a pastors' school for the training of supply pastors of the Mexican Methodist Conference.

Other Workers for the Provisional Conference

In addition to the churches and their pastors, there should be included in this brief history the persons who served the Conference as staff members. One of these is Mary Chun Lee. She served the Provisional Conference and its churches as the youth director. A Korean American layperson from Los Angeles, she served the Conference through Conference year 1950, when she resigned to get married.

In 1951 Miss Ruth Gress, a returned missionary from China, took over the youth director position. In addition to this responsibility, she spent part of her time developing a new program for teaching English to the new immigrants and refugees. After integration, Ruth worked full-time on the new project, which was called "Work with Non-English Speaking Peoples." At first this program was aimed at new Chinese immigrants. While some classes were held, one of its features was a one-to-one approach and family-to-family activities. The focus was on women newcomers. Classes were first organized in those cities where Chinese Methodist congregations existed. Women's Societies of Christian Service helped to recruit workers in neighboring non-Chinese churches. Soon the program was being adopted by other communities, and newcomers of other ethnic or language backgrounds were being helped also. Ruth Gress continued with this work until she retired in 1970.

CURRENT DEVELOPMENTS

We have been looking at the past. Let us now focus on the present. From the mid-1960s, efforts to start new Chinese churches were being made by our denomination in different parts of the country.

New York

Although Chinese ministries in New York can be dated back to the nineteenth century, no continuing congregation or church was established until the 1960s.

According to a recorded document of a missionary society of the Methodist Church, in New York's Lower East Side in 1878 L. S. Brown of Five Points Mission, with the assistance of a Cantonese ministerial student, opened an evening school for Chinese. In 1883 Mary A. Lathbury and the Methodist Chinese Mission established the Eighteenth Street Methodist Church. In 1904 Mary Banta, a Methodist missionary returned to the United States because of illness, was invited to join the Church of All Nations, at 9 Second Avenue, with a center located in Chinatown. Banta coordinated with all the agencies involved in services for the Chinese residents. She worked in this capacity for the next thirty years and retired in 1934.

After World War II and especially after the changes in immigration laws during President Kennedy's term of office, Chinese again migrated to the United States in large numbers. This was accelerated after the Communist Revolution in China, in the 1950s. The political changes that occurred in Southeast Asia from that decade to the present also contributed to this influx because many ethnic Chinese of the Philippines, Malaysia, Burma, Indonesia, Vietnam, and other nations in that part of Asia came to this country when they had to relocate.

New York, which already had one of the largest Chinese communities, was a natural point of entry for many of these newcomers. Thus in the 1960s the United Methodist City Society and the Five Points Mission began planning a ministry for the Chinese community. In 1964 there had gathered enough Chinese people to have a Chinese worship service. Bishop Lloyd C. Wicke appointed the Reverend Moses Lee as pastor, at the request of the Reverend Dr. Henry Wyman, executive secretary for the United Methodist City Society, and Miss Anita Harris, president of Five Points Mission. By 1966 the congregation was strong enough to be chartered as a church in the New York Conference of the Methodist Church.[25]

Two factors about these newcomers have a special impact in relation to Methodism in America. One of these is the fact that many of the new arrivals were already Christians. The other is that many of these newcomers spoke a variety of Chinese dialects—not just Cantonese, as was the situation a century ago, but Mandarin also. Recognizing this situation, the New York Chinese United Methodist Church has its services in both Mandarin and Cantonese. Pastor Lee speaks both and is thus able to meet the linguistic needs of both groups.

Having been a Methodist pastor from Hong Kong Conference prior to transferring to the New York Conference, Lee brought the names used by Chinese Methodists in Hong Kong and other parts of Asia. The Methodists in Hong Kong related to the Methodist Conference in Great Britain use the name Jun Dao, "Follow the Truth." The Methodists who were formerly members of Central Conferences of the Methodist Church use the name Wei-Li, "Wesley." By combining both of these into the name of the Chinese church in New York, Chinese-speaking folks from Hong Kong, Taiwan, and many other Asian countries were able to recognize it as a Methodist church.

In California, unfortunately, the Chinese Methodist churches never changed their Chinese names after the reunion of 1939 and added only the "United" in 1968 with the merger of the Evangelical-United Brethren Church and the Methodist Church. The name used was Mei Yee Mei, which was a transliteration of "M. E. Mission." For over one hundred years this name was the one used; keeping it provided the old-timers with a sense of continuity. However, it did not provide name recognition or welcome to the newcomers. New York did the appropriate thing. Since 1982, some of the California Chinese Churches have updated their name.

The Chinese church of New York City today as 334 members. Besides Moses Lee, there is one associate pastor, one parish worker, three voluntary associates, six licensed lay speakers, and one candidate for the ordained ministry attending seminary. In addition to two Sunday worship services, one in Chinese and one in English, church school, and five fellowships, the church sponsors many needed programs in the community. These include Kai Yin Radio Ministry; Community Developers; the Chinese Methodist Center, which includes a day care center; Mei Wah Chinese School Youth program; adult English classes; and the Chinese Methodist Center. These efforts provide care and services to people in the community around the church. An estimated five hundred people are served daily.[26]

Georgia

A new Chinese United Methodist Church was chartered in Decatur, Georgia, in 1984, with the Reverend Kuok-Ding Lau as pastor. While there have been a number of efforts to provide ministry to the ethnic Chinese, this was the first chartered Chinese church established by Methodists in any of the southern states.

In 1980 Miss Hilda Keng, a teacher in the area and a Methodist, had gathered three Vietnamese families and one Laotian family . . . plus others who had come from Hong Kong, Taiwan and China for Sunday worship. In 1981 Lau was transferred in from the Louisville Conference to serve the new congregation. By 1984 the congregation had developed enough strength to be regularly chartered.

Lau originally came from Malaysia and had been ordained there. Because many of the newcomers in this part of Georgia are refugees and have a very limited knowledge of English, Pastor Lau has to provide all kinds of social services as well as spiritual guidance. The church does not have facilities of its own. The Oak Grove United Methodist Church of Decatur, Georgia, is sharing its facilities with this Chinese congregation. Pastor Lau speaks Mandarin and several other Chinese dialects.[27]

Washington, D.C.

Christian ministry among the Chinese in Washington, D.C., was a united effort of several denominations for decades. This led to the establishment of the Chinese Community Church, which eventually became a part of the Association of Community Churches. The present pastor is the Reverend Dr. Man-King Tso, who is a member of the Baltimore Annual Conference under special appointment to that church. This church, however, is Cantonese speaking, as was true of all the Chinese churches in America prior to World War II. Since many Chinese who emigrated following World War II did not speak Cantonese, it was recognized that a Mandarin-speaking congregation was needed. In 1980 one was started in Chevy Chase, Maryland, a neighboring suburb of the District of Columbia. The Reverend Timothy Ang, who came from the Methodist Church of Malaysia, is the pastor.

Northern California

In Northern California, two previously all-white churches have become churches served by Chinese American pastors. This was done with intention, so that they might offer a ministry to the Chinese people who now live in large numbers near those churches.

One of these churches is located in San Francisco, First St. John's United Methodist Church. First St. John's had been two different and separate churches: old First Church and the former Italian-speaking church known as St. John's. The need for an Italian-speaking church had passed many years ago. As the makeup of the neighborhoods around both churches changed, their memberships declined. People of Italian ancestry no longer concentrated in the vicinity of St. John's Methodist Church. In the neighborhood around First Methodist Church, there had been a steady decline for years of white families with young children. The two churches merged, and the facilities of First Church became the home for the combined congregation.

In the neighborhood around First St. John's, the number of Chinese families with young children was growing rapidly. In actuality it had become the residential part of Chinatown. Two other denominations already have thriving Chinese congregations near first St. John's. Bishop R. Marvin Stuart and his cabinet decided that appointing a pastor who could serve both the then predominantly white congregation and the Chinese American community around the church would be the strategic thing to do. The pastor of First St. John's at that time was the Reverend Robert Stewart, a white man. Stewart had already opened the doors of the church to house the Hip Wo School, which was a joint project of The United Methodist Church and the

Congregational Church of Chinatown. In 1980 the Reverend Benjamin Fong transferred from the Methodist Church of Hong Kong and was appointed to First St. John's.

The other church is Riverside United Methodist Church in Sacramento. This had been an Evangelical-United Brethren Church. The neighborhood around this church had a heavy Chinese population. As had been the experience of other churches in changing neighborhoods, the white congregation was getting smaller. The pastors who served this church had tried for a number of years to reach out to the Chinese residents in the area but without much success.

In 1972 Bishop Charles F. Golden appointed the Reverend Man-King Tso to serve both Riverside Church and the Chinese church. When Tso went to Washington, D.C., to serve the Chinese Community Church there, he was followed by the Reverend Calvin Wong who came from the United Church in Hong Kong. Both of these pastors attempted to bring about a merger of the two churches. Their attempts were not successful, although some of the people of the Chinese United Methodist Church did transfer their memberships to Riverside Church.

The Reverend Mo Chi Huang, a native of Hong Kong, has been pastor of Riverside Church since 1983. She had entered the ministry in the California-Nevada Conference in 1979 and served other appointments before this one. Riverside Church offers a number of service programs for newcomers, including classes in English as a second language.

In 1983 the Chinese caucus of the California-Nevada Conference became concerned about ministering to the growing Chinese community in the area bordering the southern end of San Francisco Bay. The several Chinese congregations in the Conference contributed to a fund to start work with the use of the chapel in First United Methodist Church of San Jose. Lay persons and pastors, especially of the Oakland and San Francisco churches, assisted by conducting services. Subsequently, a Chinese pastor on leave of absence from the Singapore Conference has been serving the group. Because most of the people who have been responding live near the city of Fremont, the group has since moved to meet at the First United Methodist Church of Fremont. This work has not yet become chartered as a church.[28]

Southern California

It is in southern California that more new work among Chinese has been started than anywhere else in the country. This has been largely due to the vision and leadership of the Reverend Leo Hsu. He came from Hong Kong to serve the newly organized Orange County Chinese United Methodist Church in 1977.

With the encouragement of Joseph Ma, then the pastor, several families of the Chinese church of Los Angeles gathered together to prayerfully consider starting a church for the Chinese who live in Orange County east of Los Angeles. They had moved out to Orange County and felt the need for a Chinese church closer to where they live. Hsu, who was in this country studying at that time, was contacted and agreed to come. In 1978 the church was chartered.

When Ma retired, Hsu was appointed to the Chinatown church of Los Angeles. The Reverend Timothy Ting was then appointed to the new congregation and served it from 1979 to 1985. Presently, the Reverend David Tsang is pastor.

Presently, the Chinese church in Los Angeles and the Chinese church in Orange County are the two churches which are chartered and self-supporting, but the Los Angeles church is the only one with its own facilities. The Orange County church is sharing the facilities of the Tustin United Methodist Church.

There are three other places where ministry to Chinese residents has been inaugurated. One of these is at Alhambra First Church, where Timothy Ting is the associate pastor. Another is at the San Gabriel United Methodist Church, with the Reverend Emmanuel Wu from the Taiwan Methodist Church as minister to the Chinese. A third one is at Pomona Valley, where the Reverend Kao Fong Yip is pastor. Mandarin Chinese is the language used at all three in conducting worship. They are not yet chartered churches but are outreach ministries to Chinese people with the help of the California-Pacific Conference and the local churches in whose building they are meeting. Some Chinese have joined the host congregation as members. Others are constituents.[29]

Chinese American Pastors

In recent decades, Chinese American pastors are serving in many of the Annual Conferences throughout this country. One of them is the Reverend Dr. George Wang, who is a district superintendent in the Northern New Jersey Conference. Prior to coming to the United States, Dr. Wang was the principal of Trinity Theological College in Singapore.

CONCLUSIONS

As we review the history of Chinese United Methodist churches, it is evident that their growth in numbers and membership is linked with immigration of Chinese people into the United States. With the passage of time and the addition of American-born and American-educated younger generations, there came changes. The most obvious change is the use of the English language in teaching and in public worship. Most of our churches have bilingual services; a few have separate English and Chinese services. In a few of our churches more than one dialect of Chinese is used as well.

As we look to the future, it is difficult to predict what these churches will be like. Residentially, Chinese families live wherever they wish and are financially able to acquire dwelling places. However, even American-born and American-educated Chinese retain a taste for Chinese food, so Chinatowns may still exist indefinitely, especially in metropolitan areas where there are Chinese in large numbers. Since most of these have had Chinese churches, these churches may continue to provide a distinctive ministry. Those churches that are located in areas or cities that do not have a continuing, visible Chinese community will likely go the same route as some of the missions of the early twentieth century.

As one who has roots that touch on the early history of our Chinese churches and has been active in the contemporary scene until recently, it is with appreciation that the author recalls the many workers—white and Chinese, clergy and lay—and especially the many volunteers who have had a Christian concern for our people. It is also good to note the positive response of Chinese Americans to the call of Christ to be his disciples.

NOTES

1. *Journal of the California Annual Conference,* 1865, 1866, 1867.

2. Otis Gibson, *The Chinese in America* (Cincinnati: Hitchcock & Walden, 1877).

3. Hon Fan Chan, "History of Chinese Methodism on the Pacific Coast," *The California Christian Advocate,* Oct. 26, 1926, p. 2.

4. Gibson, *Chinese in America.*

5. Chan, *"History of Chinese Methodism,"* p. 2.

6. Sumio Koga (compiler), *A Centennial Legacy, History of Japanese Missions in North America* (Chicago: Nobart, Inc., 1977).

7. Edwar Lee, "Pacific Chinese Mission," in *Encyclopedia of Methodism,* vol. 2, ed. Bishop Nolan B. Harmon (Nashville: United Methodist Publishing House, 1974), p. 1842.

8. Ibid.

9. Gibson, *Chinese in America,* p. 201.

10. Ibid.

11. Ibid.

12. "History of Gum Moon," one-page mimeographed promotional flyer for the Gum Moon Women's Residence Hall in 1985.

13. Lucinda Glenn, "Discovery Made at Gum Moon", an unpublished manuscript telling about the discovery of Superintendent Carrie G. Davis's unpublished journal, *Record of Work in Oriental Home from February 1903.* Available from Gum Moon Women's Residence Hall, 940 Washington St., San Francisco, CA 94108.

14. Hazel M. Romahn, "A Brief History of the Origin and Development of Gum Moon Residence Hall," unpublished paper of the Memorial Committee, May 1973. Available from Gum Moon Women's Residence Hall: see note 13 for address.

15. Guangdong is the contemporary spelling of the name of the province in China that used to be spelled Kwangtung. Canton is the capital of that province and gives its name to the dialect of Chinese considered "official" in the Chinese communities in the United States. It is from this province in southern China that practically all of the first immigrants from China came.

16. Wesley S. Woo, "Protestant Work among the Chinese in the San Francisco Bay Area, 1850–1920" (Ph.D. diss., Graduate Theological Union, Berkeley, California, 1983).

17. *Journal of the California Annual Conference,* 1901, p. 86.

18. James Bashford, "Chinese Methodists in Kwangtung Province, China," *California Christian Advocate,* Aug. 5, 1901, p. 59.

19. *Journal of the Pacific Chinese Mission Conference,* 1915, pp. 21-23.

20. *Journal of the California Oriental Mission Conference,* 1939.

21. *Discipline of The Methodist Church* (Nashville: United Methodist Publishing House, 1944), par. 1850.

22. *Journal of the California Oriental Provisional Conference,* 1948, p. 18.

23. The Filipino and Korean churches are mentioned here only. Their histories appear elsewhere in this book.

24. The material for this section came from the writer's own memory, materials in the *Journal of the California Oriental Provisional Conference,* interviews with the pastors mentioned, and correspondence.

25. *Chinese United Methodist Church 15th Anniversary Journal,* New York, 1981.

26. Moses Lee, letter to Wilbur Choy, Oct. 1, 1985.

27. Kuok-Ding Lau, "Chinese United Methodist Church," *Southeast Jurisdictional Conference Report,* 1984.

28. The material for this portion came from the files of the writer, who served the California-Nevada Annual Conference as its resident bishop from 1980 to 1984.

29. The material for this portion came from an interview with the Reverend Leo Hsu.

C H A P T E R 5

GATHERING OF THE SCATTERED:

History of Filipino American United Methodist Churches

Artemio R. Guillermo

Israel, remember this! The Lord—and the Lord alone—is our God. Love the Lord your God with all your heart, with all our soul, and with all your strength. Never forget these commands that I am giving you today. Teach them to your children. Repeat them when you are at home and when you are away, when you are resting and when you are working.

(Deuteronomy 6:4-7 GNB)

CHRISTIANITY IN THE PHILIPPINES

Christianity was introduced to the Philippine Islands by Roman Catholic priests after Ferdinand Magellan, a Portuguese soldier of fortune sailing under the Spanish flag, claimed the islands in the name of King Phillip II on March 16, 1521. Subsequent conquistadores subdued the petty kingdoms on various islands until full sovereignty was established, and the archipelago was christened the Philippine Islands. For almost four hundred years Spain governed the islands as a political and economic colony. Spaniards held almost all positions of authority and owned vast tracts (*haciendas*) of fertile agricultural lands. As can be expected, Roman Catholicism was the state religion. Filipinos were either converted and coerced to join the church on pain of eternal damnation. No other religion was allowed to thrive. Civil rights for the native population were nonexistent. All throughout the Spanish rule the Filipinos were hardly exposed to the teachings of Protestant faiths.

When the Spanish-American War of 1898 ended, Filipinos started hearing the good news from American soldiers turned erstwhile preachers to an expectant and hungry people. Like a prairie wildfire, Protestant Christianity spread rapidly over the hills and valleys of the chain of seven thousand islands. After work was begun by the evangelical missions in 1899, representatives of the Presbyterian, Methodist Episcopal, and United Brethren missions formed the Evangelical Union of the Philippines in April 1901. A comity agreement was drawn up to avoid conflict and competition among the various missionary bodies. Later on Baptist, Congregational, and Christian missions joined the nation.

The comity agreement lasted until 1946 when the Philippine Federation of Christian Churches (National Council of Christian Churches) formally dissolved the comity agreement, which was no longer tenable with the arrival of fundamentalist and Pentecostal sects. The Philippines then became an open field for spreading the seeds of evangelical faith.

IMMIGRATION TO HAWAII

Following the debacle of Spanish colonial government in the Philippines in 1899 at the hands of American expeditionary forces, Filipinos started trickling into the United States through Hawaii in 1906. Most of the early immigrants were unlettered laborers recruited by the Hawaii Sugar Planters' Association to work the lush sugar and pineapple fields of the balmy islands. In a span of forty years, the trickle became a downpour as some 109,513 people flooded this labor-intensive industry.

The majority of these Filipinos professed the Roman Catholic religion but were nominal in practice. Many of them saw the church as the place to be only during critical junctures in their lives, such as baptism, weddings, and funerals.

While migrations to Hawaii were going on, the Methodist Episcopal Church was also sending American missionaries to the island of Luzon (Philippines). The first Protestant sermon heard in Manila was delivered by Bishop James M. Thoburn of India on March 5, 1899.[1] This man of God was on his way back to the United States when he learned of the defeat of the Spaniards in the Philippines and decided to call on Manila and assess the possibilities of missionary service there.

Among the early converts to the Methodist faith was Nicolas Zamora, who was ordained deacon by Bishop Thoburn on March 10, 1900. By this act the brilliant Tagalog preacher became the first licensed Filipino Methodist minister in the Philippines. His assignment was a growing congregation that became the predecessor of what is now known as Knox Memorial United Methodist Church, considered the flagship of Philippine Methodists. The church claims the biggest membership of all United Methodist churches in the islands.

Nurtured by generous support from the Methodist Episcopal Church in the United States and fired by the zeal of the missionaries, Methodism flourished in Luzon. People flocked to street meetings and open air gatherings in town squares to hear Methodist preachers. This revival preaching, called *culto pentecostal*, often lasted for a week to ten days. Proclaiming Christ boldly in an often hostile crowd, preachers called people to repent of their sins and urged them to strive toward Christian perfection. Evangelism was a year-round church activity, which brought in a rich harvest of souls into the fold of the church. Membership in the Methodist Episcopal Church in the Philippines peaked during the decades of the 1930s and 1940s.

Meanwhile, the mission office of the church in Philadelphia was not unaware of Filipino laborers in Hawaii. Six years after the arrival of the first batch of labor recruits, the Filipino Mission was established, and ministry to Filipino laborers was opened in three fronts: rural plantations, a school for boys, and the city of Honolulu.

One enterprising Filipino, Benito Ilustre, saw the unhappy plight of his compatriots and offered himself as a preacher of the Good News. Dr. John W. Wadman, superintendent of the Hawaii Mission, immediately appointed him a local preacher, since Ilustre had just completed his first year of theological studies at the Pacific School of Religion at Berkeley, thus making him the first licensed Filipino minister in Hawaii. Another Filipino felt the calling to preach, Mariano Guerrero, who was received on trial in the California Conference under which the Hawaii Mission was administered.

HAWAII MISSION TO FILIPINOS

As the Hawaii mission to Filipinos grew, more programs were offered to meet their needs. Epworth League meetings were held on Sunday afternoons. In the evenings there was an adult education school. The mission functioned as an employment bureau to help those who were laid off. There was also a flourishing religious literature program. The mission station on Queen Street in Honolulu became known as the "headquarters" to Filipinos. It was the place for socializing with fellow homesick countrymen. Since most of them had no families, the headquarters was the place to while away boring hours of inactivity.

When Sunday worship services at the Queen Street church began attracting an overflowing crowd, it became necessary to move to another building on the corner of Hotel and River streets in Honolulu. During the week the ministers conducted vesper and Bible studies, which were well attended by gospel-hungry laborers. To handle the expanded work of the mission, Rudolph Zurbuchen, a German Methodist preacher, was appointed full-time pastor of the headquarters. His report on Filipino work for the year past showed that there were 12,000 to 15,000 Filipinos in the islands and that they were coming at the rate of 500 a month. To help Zurbuchen, the mission assigned Ilustre to the Queen Street congregation and sent Guerrero to the developing Aiea congregation. Preaching stations were also established in Waimanalo, Aiea, Kahuku, Makaweli, Eleele, and Waimea.

Preaching of the Word was delivered in the native tongues of the Filipinos, who were mostly Tagalog and Visayan speaking (the Ilocano workers came later); therefore, the Hawaii Mission had to recruit preachers from the Philippines. This posed some major difficulties because the preachers were also badly needed in the expanding Methodist ministry in Philippine provinces. Besides, it was not too easy to attract preachers to Hawaii since they couldn't bring their families. However, God spoke to a few intrepid souls like Victorio Fajardo, Roman Umipig, Juan Capanas, Cenon Ramos, and Simeon Amor. Their faithful witness and preaching brought in many conversions to Jesus Christ. Zurbuchen was glowing in his report in the 1913 official minutes of the Hawaii Mission:

> We ought to go forward with this work of the Filipino Mission, because we have already commenced it; because we should preserve the work already done by our Missionaries in the Philippines; because we ought to reach the thousands yet untouched by the Gospel Light; and we ought to train here under favorable circumstances a company of such workers, who afterwards shall go to their homes and spread the message of Salvation.[2]

One of the prosperous ministries was the congregation in Honolulu. After several moves to places where the growing congregation could be accommodated, the group finally organized themselves as the Filipino United Church in 1923. The new church was jointly supported by the Congregational and Methodist missions. The union lasted for thirty years, until 1953 when the church became the Aldersgate Methodist Church. Following the union of the Evangelical United Brethren and the Methodist Church in 1968, the church's name was changed to Aldersgate United Methodist Church, which has produced many active Methodist laypersons.

There was very little family life among the early Filipino Methodists, owing to the policy of the plantation to discourage bringing family members. So the laborers were free to move about from one plantation to another at the close of a planting season. Their mobility affected the attendance of worshiping communities in many camps. In 1921 there were eighteen preaching stations located in the following islands: Oahu (seven), Kauai (four), Maui (three), Hawaii (four). To minister to these stations, there were eleven exhorters and preachers, four nurses, and two Bible women (i.e., deaconesses).[3] Although the Filipinos arrived at Hawaii later than the Japanese and Koreans, they had more preaching stations than the others had. Indeed, Filipino congregations were the fastest growing in Hawaii, and Filipinos constituted the second largest ethnic group in the islands.

All of the ethnic congregations were tied wholly to the fortunes of the sugar and pineapple industries. Their connections were severed when the world market price of these commodities began to drop in the late 1920s, forcing the industry to cut its labor force. The price erosion culminated in the great market crash of 1929. Thousands of workers were laid off, and many of them found their way to the mainland United States to work on the vegetable and fruit farms of California. Some were drawn to the fish canneries of Alaska and Washington.

The migration of Filipino laborers to the mainland not only affected the membership of the church in various islands but also forced the Hawaii Mission to follow a strategy of retrenchment for the remaining Filipino-language congregations. Several congregations were phased out. The official journal of the Hawaii Mission of 1930 showed that there still were thirteen preaching stations; these were reduced to eleven by 1934. The attrition continued up to the start of World War II, when war-related industries in the mainland beckoned for laborers, leading to another mass exodus. Many draft-age Hawaii-born Filipinos were taken into the armed forces of Uncle Sam to fight in Europe and Southeast Asia.

Today, there are seven predominantly Filipino congregations in the Hawaii District; four have ordained Filipino ministers, and the rest are served by Anglo (white) ministers. The Kaumakani United Methodist Church (formerly Makaweli Methodist Church) is the oldest existing Filipino Methodist church in the United States and is also the oldest Methodist church building in Hawaii. It was organized June 30, 1913.[4]

CHRISTIAN WORK ON THE MAINLAND

The stock market crash did not deter the immigration of Filipinos to the West Coast. Hundreds landed in San Francisco, the port of entry for immigrants; often some two to four hundred Filipinos would travel in a single vessel. On hand to meet the new arrivals were the husband and wife team of Mr. and Mrs. W. P. Stanley, who served as guardian angels as they steered many from unscrupulous white labor contractors and brought them to safe and wholesome places.

At the peak point of immigration, there were six to seven thousand Filipinos living in the Bay region. Stanley, who was pastor of the Howard Street Methodist Church, invited the Filipinos to the church for prayer and fellowship. As more Filipinos showed up at the meetings, he organized the group as the Filipino Christian Fellowship in 1920. That year marked the beginning of eighteen years of fruitful ministry. Those years were highlighted by the group's movement from one place to another—eleven times, as it sought a place to worship. Finally, the Board of Missions and Church Extension granted funds to purchase a property on Pine Street. For the first time in twenty years, the church and its pastor, Placido Palmejar (who became minister when the Stanleys retired in 1939), moved into a building of their own. The following year, Ermie Obien took over as minister, and the fellowship became known as Filipino Community Methodist Church. The thirty-ninth session of the California Oriental Mission was held at the church.

Across the bay, a similar fellowship of Filipinos was thriving under the leadership of Amadeo Fayloga. This group met temporarily in a renovated storeroom on Franklin Street, until more suitable quarters were found on West Street. The sanctuary was a church building built for a black congregation that had become insufficient for the needs of the owners. Fayloga was also involved in opening Methodist work among Filipinos in Vallejo, where many Filipinos worked in the naval yards. Because Fayloga had to find outside work in order to live and also had to finish his studies at the Pacific School of Religion at Berkeley, the work in Vallejo was slow. However, with the appointment of Eugenio Marquez as assistant pastor, there was a remarkable increase in worship attendance.

In Stockton Filipino work was going on in earnest under Pio Julian Daba. A place of worship was found with the help of Mr. and Mrs. White, former teachers in the Philippines. Although there were thousands of Filipinos in the area, a majority were of Roman Catholic faith and were quite lukewarm to evangelization work, so the work remained small. However, when Dionisio Gonzalo took over from Daba in 1943, the work picked up. Many joined the Filipino Community Church. Daba was sent to Seattle to carry on the Filipino work started there by the Bundys. Mission funds were found to provide the minister a parsonage and a community house, which served as a chapel. The community house built adjacent to the parsonage served the needs of transient Filipinos, who found it difficult to find lodging in the city.

Gonzalo's work in Stockton was enlarged into a circuit with the addition of Fresno, where work was initially under Ida Moody, a public school teacher. Because Moody's job required her full attention, the district superintendent directed Gonzalo to visit the developing congregation in Fresno.

Agustin Lopez, a Filipino layman as well as a licensed lay preacher of the Oakland Filipino congregation, saw the need of opening work among the Filipinos in El Centro. When he had a group of regular worshipers, Timoteo Baja was appointed supply pastor. Unfortunately, the work had to be abandoned when Baja had to leave his post to take a government job.

When the California Oriental Provisional Conference was organized in 1945 to replace the California Oriental Mission, there were three ethnic divisions within it: Chinese, Koreans, and Filipinos. The appointed district superintendent was Edwar Lee, pastor of the Oakland Chinese Methodist Church and the first Oriental to be in that position. The Filipinos had five charges, and their pastors were Amadeo Fayloga, (Oakland-Vallejo circuit), Eugenio Marquez (assistant pastor at Vallejo), Ermie Obien (San Francisco), Pio Julian Daba (Seattle), and Dionisio Gonzalo (Stockton-Fresno circuit).

Among the three divisions, Filipino work was the weakest because of several factors: insufficient support for the ministers, lack of places to worship, and lack of new recruits for the ministry. Edwar Lee in his report in 1946 mentioned also that the "isolation of Oriental churches" contributed to their poor state. He described the situation as follows:

> American churches hardly realize that we exist. In the past there were always Americans, both men and women, associated with our Oriental churches as teachers and workers but now less and less Americans come to the fellowships and to give resourceful help after the fashion of settlement work and thereby break down the present isolation. . . . It is sad commentary that most of our American churches find it easier to do Foreign Mission work than to do it in America.[5]

Despite his gloomy assessment, Lee's tenure was marked by acquisition of new buildings and parsonages for the Chinese, Koreans, and Filipinos. Notable gains were made in the purchase of properties where new buildings of worship were erected. The San Francisco Filipino congregation, which had moved from pillar to post five times in the last two years, found a fine church building in the heart of the Filipino district. The Seattle Filipinos remodeled their church with funds from the Mission Board. Parsonages were acquired for the ministers in Oakland, Stockton-Fresno, and San Francisco. These material improvements boosted Filipino Methodist ministry significantly.

Lest it be said that early Filipino work on the West Coast was carried on only by men, it must be mentioned that without the unselfish and devoted help of women, Methodist work among the Filipinos would not have progressed the way it did. Some of these women include Dionisia Castillo, president of Women's Society of Christian Service (WSCS) of the California Oriental Provisional Conference 1946; Maria Dayoan Garcia, secretary of religious education and young people's work, 1945 to 1946; Mrs. Helen Marquez, president, WSCS, 1950 to 1951.

NEW TYPES OF IMMIGRANTS

The granting of Philippine independence by the United States in 1946 abruptly curtailed the flow of emigrés to the United States. Labor-intensive farms and fish canneries had to use Asians from the Hawaiian plantations. Some nineteen years later a revision of the U.S. Immigration Law in 1965 liberalized quotas for immigrants from Asia. This brought profound changes in the types of immigrants. Under the new law the immigration of professionals was allowed. Thus a horde of Filipino professionals came to the United States in the late 1960s. Sociologists described this flight as a "brain drain" for the Philippines, because so many of the emigrants were skilled professionals, highly educated and achievement-oriented individuals such as medical doctors, nurses, teachers, engineers, medical technologists, accountants, and chemists. Most of them immediately found employment in urban areas in the West coast, Midwest, East, and South. Language being no barrier, since English is the medium of instruction in public schools and the official language of the government of the Philippines, the new wave of Filipino immigrants had few problems in communication and social integration.

A number of Protestant Filipinos found their way to local Methodist and community churches. In churches where there were sizable numbers of Filipinos, fellowships were organized for worship and social functions. Host churches generously provided facilities and arranged church programs to accommodate the new worshipers. In some churches in the West Coast where the Filipino presence was highly visible, the administration hired Filipinos as associate ministers and staff persons.

CAUCUSES ARTICULATE NEED

Providing impetus to the formation of Filipino United Methodist churches in the United States was the work of Filipino caucuses of the Pacific and Southwest Annual Conference, which vigorously articulated the need for more churches that would nurture their spiritual growth. The caucus movement went on a national scale in the 1970s, as other ethnic groups—Hispanics, Native Americans, Asians, and Pacific Islanders—raised their voices for recognition of their unique ministry and mission within The United Methodist Church. Church officials acknowledged the concerns of these leaders by providing funding assistance for the convocations and consultations of the ethnic groups.

Beneficiaries of this caucus movement were the old, established ethnic churches and the embryonic ethnic fellowships that were already gestating in white churches. Through the caucus movement new leaders surfaced and took the initiative of strengthening their own churches and set the footings of new churches. The United Methodist Church through General Conference action affirmed in 1976 its support for a pluralistic constituency by its quadrennial emphasis on ethnic minority local churches in 1980; the emphasis was reaffirmed in 1984 by the General Conference.

Even before the quadrennial emphasis was adopted, Asian Americans had already started their claim for self-identity as a worshiping community. This claim was not asserted without a struggle. Bishop Roy Sano, then professor at the Pacific School of Religion at Berkeley, California, cited racism as the stumbling block in liberating ethnics from their present situation as second-class citizens in the church.

While racism reared its ugly visage in the form of cultural oppression, it failed to dampen the burning zeal of Filipino Protestants to witness in their own distinct spiritual expressions. In contrast to their illiterate brethren who migrated some fifty years ago, postwar Filipino immigrants competed aggressively in the marketplace of employment while waging a valiant crusade for assimilation as members in the white-dominated church and society.

PATTERNS OF FILIPINO ASSIMILATION INTO EXISTING CHURCHES[6]

Assimilation into another culture follows a pattern. Jose Movido, a Filipino minister in the Los Angeles area who conducted a study of the development of Filipino congregations in Los Angeles for his doctoral dissertation, found that there are six patterns of minority assimilation: segregation, infiltration, confrontation, integration, compromise, and pluralism or coexistence.[7] Postwar Filipino immigrants followed the patterns of infiltration, integration, and coexistence. Filipino churches originating long before World War II started as segregated congregations, as did other Asian ethnic churches (Chinese, Japanese, and Koreans), but gradually desegregated when they were absorbed in the new structure of Annual Conferences and jurisdictions as mandated by General Conferences. The pattern of congregational develop-ment became evident as more Filipinos entered white churches, where before they were not welcomed.

In the Los Angeles area there is a substantial concentration of Filipinos: old residents, retired servicemen, and new immigrants and their families. Nine United Methodist churches in the area where these Filipinos predominate followed the Movido model, and Filipinos are now their majority constituents. Over the past decades white membership in these churches went downhill, due in part to natural attrition and to socioeconomic changes in their neighborhoods, such as an influx of Hispanics and other minorities. While Methodist churches in the Los Angeles area affirmed the presence of Filipinos among them, they were simply names on the church roll, and few of them were admitted into the inner circles of administrative councils. To many who were professionals, it was difficult to be in church and not actively involved in church life and programs. Consequently many of them lost interest in the church, and some sought membership in non-Methodist churches that made use of their talents and gifts. For those who remained, time was on their side. As their numbers grew, the church invited them to fill in positions of leadership.

Wilmington United Methodist Church

One of the churches that integrated Filipinos was the Wilmington United Methodist Church, located near the bustling naval shipyard in Long Beach.

Long before the war the church had an all-white membership of professionals and personnel from the shipyard. After the war the church had a multi-ethnic membership; the majority were Filipinos, but they waved no ethnic label. The congregation preferred it that way because they wanted an inclusive church open to all races. Indeed, the church roll showed representatives of various ethnic groups. Where the neighborhood used to be mostly Anglos, the area is now largely populated by Hispanics. As a good neighbor, Wilmington carries on a "food pantry" program as a social service to the poor and needy. Another facet of their social concern is their adult education program, which is taught by a retired and energetic school teacher who finds it a joy to teach the rudiments of the English language to Hispanics. Wilmington was cited by the Southernn California-Arizona Annual Conference (now the California-Pacific Conference) as the most "inclusive church" in the entire Conference. Their first Filipino pastor was David Pasamonte. Currently the pastor is the Reverend Melanio Loresco Jr., who will be on his thirteenth year of ministry to Wilmington.

Asbury United Methodist Church

The Filipinos at Asbury United Methodist Church on the east side of Los Angeles literally took over a dying church in 1976, when Jose Movido, Jr., began his ministry. Because there were only about ten members left, the district superintendent proposed to close the hundred-year-old church in Lincoln Heights. The structure was in disrepair and appeared to be unsafe under the city's safety codes. However, the Filipino members vigorously opposed the Conference action and passed a petition to keep the church open. With the appointment of Movido the church experienced membership growth. Unfortunately, his ministry was cut short after he suffered a stroke and became incapacitated. The ministry was carried on by Romeo del Rosario, who was finishing his thelogical studies, and Camilo Graza, a layman. Meantime, the members tried their hand at repairing the windows, roof, and grounds. At its ninety-eighth anniversary the church building was ready to receive its many guests. A new Filipino minister was sent to Asbury, Esteban Calma, who infused new vitality into the congregation by using Tagalog as the language of worship, making Asbury the only Tagalog-speaking church in southern California (Tagalog is the national language of the Filipinos). Because Los Angeles building codes required that church buildings meet earthquake standards, the Asbury congregation had to abandone their sanctuary and move to Alhambra, where they are sharing facilities with the First United Methodist Church. With a new minister, Benjamin Nicolas, the congregation is planning a new sanctuary in the foreseeable future.

Rosewood United Methodist Church

An exponent of the Movido pattern of compromise or coexistence is the Rosewood United Methodist Church. Facing North New Hampshire avenue with a commanding Gothic facade, this church traced its roots to nine laymen who met in 1904 and agreed to start a church. The church building was erected on its present site in 1925 and served a middle-class white neighborhood. It was an active and witnessing congregation when its membership peaked in the 1940s. But the construction of the Hollywood Freeway in the 1950s began to affect the area. Single-unit dwellings gave way to apartments as members moved out to the burgeoning bedroom communities of Los Angeles. Although many faithful members remained, the membership decline was irreversible.

The neighborhood and surrounding blocks changed its racial coloration. Most of the incoming residents were ethnics, (Samoans, Hispanics, Filipinos, and Koreans), and the evangelicals among them sought worship at Rosewood, and resident members welcomed them in the English service. But as the ethnics' numbers grew, it became necessary to have separate worship services in their native tongues. Soon Rosewood had a "house church" in its own sanctuary.

Among the majority ethnic worshipers at Rosewood were Filipinos. By far they outnumbered other ethnics since they started coming in the early 1960s. They began worshiping in the English service, but as their numbers leaped many of them, particularly the older persons, indicated a desire to have a Tagalog worship program. So a bimonthly afternoon service was scheduled. In the span of ten years Filipino membership at Rosewood rose dramatically, so that they became the majority in 1975. In the summer of 1975 a Filipino minister, Esteban Calma, a graduate of Fuller Theological Seminary, was appointed associate minister to serve the Filipino congregation. He served until January 1977 when he was sent to Asbury United Methodist Church as a full-time minister to the Filipinos, who took over the church by sheer majority. Calma was moved again to serve Baldwin Park United Methodist Church, where there was a growing presence of Filipinos in the multi-ethnic congregation. Josefina R. Basilio, the first Filipino clergywoman, was appointed to minister to the Filipino contingent. She was succeeded by another Filipino, Romeo del Rosario, a graduate of Boston University who became the first full-time minister of Rosewood in 1982. He served until June 1985, when he went to Sierra Leone in Africa as a missionary for the Board of Global Ministries.

For a number of Filipinos, attending Rosewood United Methodist Church in downtown Los Angeles involved a great deal of driving. Some had to travel twenty-five to forty miles to get to Rosewood. They came from such places as

Covina, La Puente, Baldwin Park, San Dimas, Azusa, and Glendora. Many families eventually dropped out and started going to the nearest church in their community. However, the Rosewood church saw the opportunity to continue their caring ministry to their former members.

The Rosewood Extension Ministry started as a proposal by the then local church lay leader, Romeo M. Abesamis, to the local church's Commission on Missions. While there were a lot of misgivings about the value of the ministry, Amado M. Umaguing, one of its proponents and an active layman, explained to those opposed to the plan that "a church to fulfill its mission in the world must continue to seek opportunities of expanding its work, even beyond geographical boundaries whenever the need arises, and be ready to die a little if only to give birth to a new fellowship."[8]

I. P. Bautista, a retired district superintendent in the Philippines, was appointed to provide oversight and leadership to the program. On December 30, 1979, the extension ministry was launched in a worship of celebration at the Covina United Methodist Church, with some 188 persons and guests in attendance. Bautista gave a stirring message titled "Our Calling in the World."

San Gabriel Valley United Methodist Church

Covina, being more accessible than Rosewood as the gathering place for scattered members, gradually emerged as the logical sponsoring congregation for the ministry. Accordingly, on Sunday, July 6, 1980, thirty-five Filipino members and constituents were received into the membership of Covina. However, while membership was held in Covina United Methodist Church, such activities as worship, adult study, and youth ministry, among others, were carried on independent of the Anglo congregation. Added to this, the ministry assumed for itself the responsibility of developing its own funding system for underwriting its operational expenses and use of facilities.

The year 1981 offered many fresh challenges. With a budget more than double that of the previous year, the Filipino ministry was carried on successfully. Since self-reliance is a vital key to ultimate self-support and financial stability, the Filipino work steadily moved toward congregational status.

In November 1982 a qualified young adult worker with the youth was added to the staff to provide leadership to the burgeoning youth population. The youth program proved to be a great boon, as young people flocked to the church.

After an arduous struggle for selfhood of little over four years, the Rosewood Extension ministry, now known as the First Filipino American United Methodist Church of San Gabriel Valley, finally received its charter as a duly organized United Methodist church of the then Pacific and Southwest Annual Conference on February 12, 1984. In ceremonies held at the Covina

United Methodist Church, the Reverend Richard V. Kendall, district superintendent, delivered the message of the afternoon, "Do You Mean Business?"

Having outgrown its quarters at the West Covina church, the Filipino congregation acquired its own sanctuary at Hillgrove United Methodist Church in Hacienda Heights, California, in 1986.

Grace United Methodist Church

In San Francisco we have the Grace United Methodist Church, whose history dates back to the Filipino Christian Fellowship mentioned earlier. Located in the Sunset district of San Francisco Bay, the congregation meets in a stucco structure straddling the intersection of Taraval and 36th Avenue, which is easily accessible by the Bay Area Rapid Transit. The district sprawls over the Pacific Ocean beach and is rich in ethnic diversity among its many retired citizens who like the gentle climate of the Bay Area. Parishioners describe Grace as the "neighborhood church on the corner."

On its sixteenth anniversary in June 1985, San Francisco mayor Diane Feinstein congratulated the congregation for its distinction as the "only Filipino United Methodist Church" in the multi-ethnic city. A majority of members are first- and second-generation Ilocanos, Tagalogs, and Visayans. However, the congregation is enriched by the presence of whites who represent the surviving members of the former Parkside Methodist Church.

Parkside had been founded in 1941 by whites at 1729 Taraval Avenue. During a span of eight years, membership blossomed to three hundred, and Sunday school classes had an attendance of some four hundred children of all ages. In the postwar years members drifted out to the burgeoning bedroom communities of the Bay Area, leaving the church high and dry. It was forced to close its doors in 1968. At about this time, the Filipino Wesley Methodist Church, formerly kown as the Filipino Community Methodist Church, was looking for a place to accommodate its growing membership. Its worship center on Pine Street was getting inadequate to handle attendance at its divine service and Sunday school. The California-Nevada Conference advised the Filipinos to seek a merger with the Parkside trustees. This was consummated on June 25, 1969, and the merged congregations adopted the new name of Grace United Methodist Church; Leonard Autajay was their minister. Juan Ancheta took over as minister in 1969 when Autajay was assigned to another church.

Social service is one of the strong community programs of Grace. The church's excellent facilities—large fellowship hall and well-furnished kitchen—are available to all the church organizations and some community groups for meetings and social functions. One of the groups meeting regularly in the social hall is the Filipino Nurses' Association of San Francisco. A social service that is greatly welcomed is the program for newly arrived Filipino immigrants. The program includes meeting them at the airport, locating housing and possibly employment, and placing their children in schools. These public relations efforts not only facilitate smooth settlement but, more importantly, endear Grace to these potential citizens. Many of the new immigrants eventually take up membership in the church.

Grace's ministry extends to the surrounding counties and nearby cities of San Francisco. Laypersons have actively assisted in developing embryo congregations in San Jose and Fresno. Today there are regularly worshiping groups in these cities. A major outpost was the Fresno Filipino American congregation, which received its charter as a church in 1988.

Beacon United Methodist Church

Like Grace United Methodist Church, Beacon United Methodist Church in Seattle, Washington, started as an ethnic congregation mostly made up of Filipino students in the area. A Filipino minister, Roman Calica, organized the students into a fellowship in 1926; they called themselves the Filipino Christian Fellowship. The fellowship was further strengthened by the Reverend and Mrs. T. Walter Bundy, former missionaries in the Philippines. Under their leadership, the students convenanted to evangelize the Filipino community and follow Christ's teaching in their daily lives. The fellowship enlarged its membership to include a cross-section of Protestants as well as whites from Europe.

The budding congregation met in the basement of First Methodist Church at 5th and Marion streets in downtown Seattle. A building fund campaign started in 1940 was augmented by a grant from the Seattle District. A vacant Japanese athletic clubhouse was purchased, and with some renovation and refurbishing the building was transformed into a house of worship. The Bundys faithfully shepherded the Filipino church until their retirement in 1945. A Filipino lay preacher, Grandino Baaoa, was appointed acting pastor and served two years. In June 1947 the Conference appointed Pio Julian Daba, who was also ordained deacon and thus became the first full-time Filipino minister.

Under Daba's tenure, the congregation was officially granted a charter as the Filipino Community Methodist Church of Seattle. On January 18, 1948, the church moved to another rented place at E. Terrace Street, one block south of the present Seattle University on 11th Avenue. Daba served until 1953 when he was called to serve the Filipino Methodist church in Oakland, California. Taking his place was Dionisio F. Gonzalo, who pastored the congregation until his retirement in 1966. Gonzalo's ministry was marked by increased membership and a high Sunday school attendance of children of all ages.

A digression is in order in this historical account. Up to 1952 the Methodist

Church had segregated congregations, conferences, and jurisdictions. The three Filipino congregations in the West Coast were mistakenly placed under the Latin American mission of the former Methodist Episcopal Church. This was later corrected when the Filipino Methodists were transferred to the California Oriental Mission of the Methodist church, which was organized in 1939. Other members of the mission were the Chinese and Korean churches.

The General Conference of the Methodist Church passed enabling legislation in 1952 that mandated the dissolution of all segregated congregations. Thereafter, all ethnic churches were absorbed in white conferences. The Filipino Community Methodist Church of Seattle came under the Seattle District of the Pacific Northwest Conference. In June 1955 the church dropped its ethnic identification to become Fellowship Methodist Church. Under this inclusive name, a new minister came on board, Stanley De Pano, a young Filipino fresh out of Garrett Theological seminary whose forebears were early converts of American Methodist missionaries in the Philippines.

Bubbling with the spirit of new wine, De Pano led his parishioners to experience an internal revival. Sunday school was revitalized with new teachers and an interesting curriculum. A choir was formed and an annual cantata instituted. Fellowship Church became highly visible in Seattle through its outreach programs, one of which was the International Drop-in Center, a social service agency that reached out to Asian Americans in the city. A remarkable increase in attendance of second-generation Filipino youth highlighted De Pano's ministry as the church became involved in the social concerns of the 1970s.

Terrace Street church facilities became inadequate as worship attendance burgeoned. Church leaders had to take a hard look at the future. Obviously, the first step was to plan a fund campaign, as they had done earlier. A novel idea of using Filipino cuisine was launched, and the response was productive. Clients were nearby churches and local organizations that welcomed ethnic dishes, albeit Filipino-style cooking.

While funds were being raised, the building committee discovered another small black church on Beacon Avenue which was in the throes of disintegration. A meeting with the Beacon Church elders led to a plan of merger, which officially took place on June 23, 1968, with the blessings of Bishop Everett W. Palmer, who granted the charter. The new congregation was christened Beacon United Methodist Church. The sanctuary was reconstructed into a more spacious worship center. De Pano had to give up his pastorate when Bishop Wilbur Choy, the newly elected episcopal leader, appointed him district superintendent to the Tacoma District. This was a signal honor for De Pano, who became the first Filipino to achieve a cabinet position in his conference. Another Filipino minister was assigned to Beacon, J. Allan Ocampo, who carried on a fruitful ministry.

With the arrival of new immigrants in the late 1970s in the Seattle area, Beacon Church further increased its membership roll. Sunday school rooms overflowed, so that the basement living quarters of the minister had to be utilized. A new parsonage was built two blocks south of the church. Also, a new position of parish associate was created, and an associate minister was appointed to help in the administration and evangelism programs. Ocampo served until June of 1980, when he was sent to Mason United Methodist Church in Tacoma as an associate minister. Miguel de Guzman, a graduate of Chicago Theological Seminary, took over the pastorate of Beacon.

Plans for a bigger sanctuary were laid out in the last year of De Guzman's appointment, when Bishop Palmer sent him to St. Paul United Methodist Church in Everett, Washington, in 1984. Construction of the new edifice began in December 1984 under Querubin D. Canlas, a former professor of Union Theological Seminary in the Philippines. His first sermon, entitled "Giants and Grasshoppers," based on Numbers 13:33, challenged the members to build a temple of God. He referred to the new project as a giant to be overcome. By setting an example in pledging, the building campaign snowballed as pledges and checks flowed into the church coffers. Helped by loans from the Board of Global Ministries and the Methodist Development Fund, the new sanctuary was completed in a year. A great deal of the labor was contributed by the members, led by Tony Sison, an engineer who was chairperson of the building committee.

Beacon continues to shed its light of hope and salvation at its little corner in the city of Seattle.

First Filipino/American United Methodist Church of Dallas

We leave the Northwest behind and continue our historical odyssey to the sprawling city of Dallas, Texas. Lucrative employment opportunities and the warm climate were some of the major attractions of this city to Filipino professionals who came to this Texas metroplex in the early 1960s. Today many of them are employed in the health care institutions and communications industry of this vital city of the Southwest.

In a quiet sector of the southeast part of Dallas sits a whitewashed chapel with a signboard announcing in script letters "First Filipino/American United Methodist Church." Note the slash mark instead of the usual hyphen in the name, to indicate the spiritual union of the Methodist heritage of Filipinos and Americans. How this valiant group of Christians found a home church is a tale of faith and vision. This church traces its beginnings to the work of three Filipino Methodist ministers: Silverio J. R. Ignacio, the venerable patriarch and retired district superintendent for the Philippines; Salvador Capuli, an ebullient young adult leader in the Philippines and an ordained Methodist minister; and Leo Tipay, Jr., a gifted young preacher with organizational abilities who immigrated to the states in the early 1970s to pursue a doctoral degree in counseling.

Using his skill in survey research, Tipay conducted an opinion survey of the religious preferences of the Filipino residents of Dallas. With the help of friends, Tipay interviewed Filipinos he met randomly in grocery stores, institutions, streets, and offices, representing a cross-section of professionals, blue- and white-collar workers, retirees, and students. When the data were tabulated, the findings indicated that an overwhelming number favored the organization of an all-Filipino congregation. Thus Tipay sent out invitations to a number of evangelicals to come for a worship service on March 4, 1979, at Stephen's United Methodist Church in Mesquite.

Thirty-seven faithful souls showed up for worship on that cold, blustery Sunday. These worshipers formed a fellowship and vowed to continue as a worshiping group. As the fellowship settled to a core group, the three ministers arranged to move their Sunday worship to a more centrally located place at Munger United Methodist Church in downtown Dallas. The church gave them the use of the basement chapel for their morning divine worship. The three ministers alternated in leading the worship, since two of them held secular jobs. Every Sunday brought new faces as each worshiper invited a friend or a relative. A program of Bible studies was conducted in homes, and pastoral visitations and telephone calls were carried out to follow up on visitors and prospective worshipers.

Since a great number of the regular worshipers were singles, Tipay organized a singles club as an outreach program to enable people to know one another in wholesome activities. During the three years that the club lasted, the activities included Bible studies, a discotheque, and social services. Meeting once a month in the social hall of the church, the club was instrumental in increasing the members of the Filipino worshipers at Munger. Through its new arrivals committee, club members were assigned turns to meet new Filipino arrivals at the airport. Basic needs were provided for, such as finding living quarters, donating initial food supplies, and locating schools for the children.

Surprisingly, club activities attracted a lot of white and black singles in Dallas, and as expected, romances developed, some of which led to successful marriages. Several were cross-cultural unions. Wedding receptions were usually potluck style, and one of the three ministers was always available for this occasion, *gratis et amore*.

Soon the fledgling congregation of Filipinos at Munger was ready to flex its wings. The group had met the requirements for a local church set forth in the Methodist *Discipline*. On July 27, 1981, Bishop John Russell of the Dallas-Ft. Worth episcopal area granted their charter as the First Filipino/American United Methodist Church of Dallas. Appointed minister on a part-time basis was Phillip Del Rosario, who also worked as a pastoral counselor in a local hospital. In view of the new status of the Filipino congregation, Munger deemed it proper to collect user fees. The Filipinos considered it time for them to look for a place they could call their own.

As God guided the wandering Israelites to the promised land, so were the Filipinos led to Glendale United Methodist Church, which was closing its doors in 1982 because of severe membership loss. The Conference offered the church building to the First Filipino/American congregation. Although the building was in a state of disrepair, the Filipinos accepted the offer, and with every member pitching in for a major spruce-up job, the building was transformed into a postcard picture of a lovely chapel set amidst a background of verdant lawn and stately elms.

Their first Sunday worship resounded with joyous singing and the joyful sounds of a string orchestra called Sanlahi Rondalla. First Filipino/American United Methodist Church is probably the only ethnic church in the denomination with its own string band. Directed by Eduardo Del Leon, a retired music teacher from the Philippines, the band is the church's major public relations tool. Since the word got around Dallas about the superb music of this all-Filipino ensemble, they have frequently been invited to play before civic and church organizations, not only in the Dallas-Ft. Worth area but also in other places in Texas.

First Filipino/American Church celebrated their fourth anniversary in July 1985 with a full-time minister. Eduardo C. Cajiuat, a former district superintendent in Manila, who came to Dallas in 1984 on an exchange pulpit arrangement with Del Rosario. The appointment was made permanent in 1985 when he was accepted as a full member of the North Texas Conference. An indefatigable worker, Cajiuat, whose nickname is Ding, has welded the congregation into a loving and caring group of Christians.

First Filipino/American Church has another distinction as an ethnic church. It is the only chartered Filipino church with a clearly stated theology and mission. Del Rosario led a retreat of the administrative board one weekend in January 1985, and out of that meeting came this statement:

> We the First Filipino/American United Methodist Church empowered by the Holy Spirit are a caring congregation, who in expression of our commitment to Jesus Christ as Saviour and Lord and seeking to grow in His grace, will reach out to others through witness and service in order that they too may experience the love of God in Christ and become his disciples.[9]

Their caring ministry has been expressed in many projects and programs beyond the church, such as providing seed money to start a mushroom industry among poor farmers in the Philippines, scholarships for nurses in a Methodist hospital in Manila and support for Phillip and Espie Del Rosario in their three-year missionary work in Greater Manila. It is the long-range plan of this young congregation to develop other Filipino congregations in the North Texas Conference.

First Filipino/American United Methodist Church of Houston

Another growing Filipino congregation in Texas is the First Filipino/ American United Methodist Church of Houston. The beginnings of this church go back to a Thanksgiving Day service on November 25, 1980, held in the home of Tony and Betty Gonzales. In attendance were members of six families who longed for the traditional church service and get-together meetings observed in the home country. The service was led by Jorge Rubio, a United Church of Christ minister. After their meeting the families voted to continue meeting as a worshiping group in homes, and Rubio volunteered to lead a Bible study and serve as interim minister. This group identified itself as the United Church of Greater Houston. However, as the number of worshipers grew, the leaders decided to identify with the Methodist tradition. A petition was sent to Bishop Finis A. Crutchfield of the Houston area asking that the United Church of Greater Houston be constituted as a local Methodist Church. When the congregation met the requirements of the Methodist *Discipline,* their charter as a duly organized church was granted on December 27, 1981. Their name became the First Filipino/American United Methodist Church, and they started worshiping at St. Matthew's United Methodist Church in Houston.

In 1982 Leo V. Tipay, Jr., was appointed supply minister. Although he ministered to the congregation on a part-time basis since he held a full-time job as hospital counselor in Dallas, the church continued to grow in membership and stewardship. In August 19, 1984, the congregation dedicated its own house of worship at Sweetwater Drive. Bishop Benjamin R. Oliphint was on hand to lead in the dedication and observance of the fifth anniversary of the Filipino congregation. The bishop described the growth of the church as a "marvelous venture of faith." With a seating capacity of 225, the Filipino/American United Methodist Church is adequately provided to minister to the spiritual needs of Filipinos in Houston. Reggie Dancel, Jr., was appointed supply pastor in 1986. Under his leadership, the congregation is in the process of relocating to a five-acre lot in the southwest area, where the majority of Filipinos live. Plans are underway to put up the First Filipino Community Center of Houston to meet the spiritual, social, and economic needs of the Filipino community.

United Filipino Church of Chicago

Our analogy of the ancient Israelites has again a bearing with the evangelical Filipinos in the Chicago area. Like their wandering ancestors, the Filipinos in this midwestern city have been wanderers for a permanent "home church." In the past ten years the United Filipino Church of Chicago (UFCC) has moved twice in its quest for a worship center of its own.

The UFCC began meeting as a worshiping community way back in 1977. They started as a Tagalog language worship group. Leading the congregation were three Filipino ministers who guided the group when they started their worship services at the Jose Rizal Center in Irving Park and later on when they moved to Galewood Community Church in 1978.

In 1980 their numbers were decimated by the migration of many members to the Sun Belt region. However, the remaining members faithfully held together. Their numbers began to increase when young Filipino professionals started joining when the worship service began being conducted in English to welcome non-Tagalog speaking people. In 1983 the UFCC, which had started as an independent and unaffiliated congregation, decided to join the connectional structure of United Methodism. The church was accepted as a mission church of the Northern Illinois Annual Conference.

Under the umbrella of the Conference, the UFCC received the benefits of its resources and leadership. The Reverend Victor Fujiu, then a district superintendent, saw to it that the mission church obtain the full support of the Conference. He also found a church in Oak Park that was fated to die unless a transplant of new members was immediately received, St. John's United Methodist Church in Oak Park, Illinois, a suburban community of Chicago. Of the original congregation of three hundred members, only eight stalwarts were left in 1984 to see the sun almost set on their weather-worn sanctuary. Attrition and major changes in the social and economic fabric of the community are some of the factors leading to the present state of affairs.

The beautiful Gothic brick edifice was built in 1916 by German-speaking members. At the end of World War I membership grew when new German immigrants found the church. Facilities were enlarged to handle the increased constituency. However, some thirty years later the once-thriving congregation experienced declining attendance when members left and the neighborhood slowly turned into a business center.

The Conference, through the Reverend Joe Agne, brought the leaders of the Filipino congregation for a meeting with the surviving leaders of St. John's. Out of the meeting came the plan for a merger. The membership transplant that St. John's desperately needed came in the form of Filipinos. The once-dying congregation came to life with one hundred Filipino hearts. They dropped their United Filipino Church of Chicago name and voted to keep St. John's United Methodist Church—but with a subtitle: Filipino-American Church. With a monetary grant from the Conference, the timeworn structure was repaired and refurbished. Roger T. Pangilinan was officially assigned as the first minister of the reconstituted church. The wandering Filipino congregation had at last found their home church.

St. John's is the flagship church of Filipino American Methodists in the Midwest. Pangilinan, a former United Church of Christ minister in the Philippines, is a graduate of Philippine Christian University, Union Theological Seminary, and Princeton Theological Seminary and held pastorates in local churches in his home country. He settled in Chicago with his family and took a secular job, while serving as a part-time minister to the Filipino congregation. In 1983 he accepted an invitation by the Northern Illinois Conference to serve as full-time minister of the mission church and continued to serve the Filipinos at their new home church in Oak Park. His training in church growth and development played a major role in laying the foundation of a thriving ethnic church in the heartland of America.

CONCLUSIONS

Since this historical account was written in 1987, several other Filipino congregations have been organized on the West Coast. Surely the growth of Filipino American churches bodes well for the future of The United Methodist Church. Fundings from the Ethnic Minority Local Church program contributed immensely to the organization of the churches. However, The United Methodist Church has had experiences with earlier ethnic churches, such as the German-speaking Methodist churches in the Midwest, which, like the old soldier, faded away into glory. With a new generation of Filipino leaders who are surfacing in many of these ethnic churches, there is a strong indication that Filipino-American churches will thrive in the richly pluralistic environment of The United Methodist Church.

The potential for developing more Filipino churches in the United States is great. There are a number of cities that remain unexplored for future church growth, such as St. Louis, Norfolk, New York, Newark, and Charleston. The call of Macedonia is ringing in these places. But this call remains unheeded, for as the Bible says, many are called but few are chosen. Thus the immediate need of Filipino United Methodist churches is for trained workers, both clergy and laity. The United Methodist Church has to be intentional in its recruitment and training of ethnics. Filipino churches also could help in identifying candidates for the ministry.

Taking a cue from our black colleagues, the Filipino clergy now serving ethnic congregations should define their theology for being. The task ahead is an articulation of a theological framework for understanding and undergirding Filipino witness in the light of God's injunctions. As William Mamoru Shinto warns, the very existence of a religious institution and the ethnic ministers within it depends in the long run on a lucid theological foundation. Bishop Roy Sano adds that Asian Americans have to define a Christian theology devoid of Western trappings.[10]

Like the ancient Israelites who wandered in the wilderness, Filipinos in America are still in their faith journey as they gather together in their own houses of worship to witness in their own distinct cultural identity for their Lord and Savior Jesus Christ.

NOTES

1. Dionisio D. Alejandro, *From Darkness to Light* (Manila: Central Conference, United Methodist Church), p. 17.

2. Rudolph Zurbuchen, "Report of the Filipino Work," in *Official Minutes of the Eighth Session of the Hawaii Mission of the Methodist Episcopal Church,* Feb. 27 to Mar. 2, 1913, p. 21. (Material deposited at Drew University Library, Madison, NJ).

3. Ibid., p. 9.

4. Alex R. Vergara, "Filipino Ministry: Past, Present and Future" (D. Min. diss., School of Theology, University of California at Claremont, 1986).

5. Edward Lee, "A Brief History of the Pacific Chinese Mission," in *Retrospection and Projection 10th Anniversary 1985* (San Francisco: National Federation of Asian American United Methodists, 1985), p. 5.

6. At the time this article was being researched, the author had no access to historical materials relating to the following churches: Fellowship United Methodist Church, Vallejo, California; Melrose United Methodist Church, Oakland, California; Geneva Avenue United Methodist Church, San Francisco, California; South Gate United Methodist Church, South Gate, California; and Daly City United Methodist Church, Daly City, California. Since this book went to press, two new Filipino United Methodist churches have been chartered: Grace United Methodist Church, Plano, Texas (an offspring of the First Filipino/American United Methodist Church, Dallas, Texas) and the Fresno Christian Fellowship in Fresno, California.

7. Jose Movido, "Co-Existence as a Strategy for Ethnic Empowerment in the American Church" (D.Min. diss., School of Theology, University of California at Claremont, 1976).

8. Interview with Amado M. Umaguing on July 16, 1985, in Los Angeles.

9. Minutes of the administrative board, Jan. 15, 1985, First Filipino/American United Methodist Church, Dallas, Texas.

10. Roy Sano, comp., *The Theologies of Asian Americans and Pacific Peoples: A Reader* (Berkeley, Calif.: Asian Center for Theology and Strategies, Pacific School of Religion, 1976), p. 283.

C H A P T E R 6

PERSECUTION, ALIENATION, AND RESURRECTION:

History of Japanese Methodist Churches

Lester E. Suzuki

PERIOD OF THE FIRST SUPERINTENDENT, MERRIMAN COLBERT HARRIS

In November 1873 the first four Methodist Episcopal Church missionary couples were sent to Japan to establish missions in Yokohama, Tokyo, Nagasaki, and Hakodate. The missionaries' endeavors would eventually lead to the formation of the Japan Methodist Church, which later was the source of many ministers going to the United States to serve Japanese Methodist churches there.

Among the missionaries were a young American couple, the Reverend and Mrs. Merriman Colbert Harris, who would eventually play critical roles in fostering Methodism among Japanese in the United States. M. C. Harris was born in Beallsville, Ohio, on July 9, 1846, and served for two years in the Union Army during the Civil War. He attended Scio College, taught school for a while, and, once he had his license to preach, served two churches by 1869. That same year he went to Allegheny College in Meadville, Pennsylvania, for further training, graduating in 1873. While there he met and married Flora Best, a poetry writer.

Through zeal and perseverance the couple founded the Hakodate Church in late 1874 (this church celebrated its hundredth anniversary in 1974). Harris was then asked to serve as American vice consul and later as consul at Hakodate. He made frequent trips to Sapporo, capital of Hokkaido, where he preached to the famous Sapporo Band, a group of young Christian students. Many of these young men were baptized by Harris; they included many who were to become notable leaders in Japan, such as Nitobe Inazo and Uchimura Kanzo. Flora Best Harris was busy on her own; she founded a girls' school, which is today known as Iai Girls' School.

Due to his wife's frail health, Harris was transferred to the second Tokyo

Circuit, the Azabu District, in 1878. The couple served there until 1886, when, again for reasons of health, Harris was sent to San Francisco to become the superintendent of what was to become the Pacific Japanese Mission. There he met Kanichi Miyama a young Japanese Methodist who was to be his partner in reaching out to immigrant Japanese. The two are credited with laying the foundations for almost all the Japanese American churches in the United States.

Miyama was the son of a samurai family and a graduate of a progressive school run by Yoshida Shoin in Hagi, Yamaguchi Ken, in western Japan. This school, and the few others like it in the country, was opposed to the isolationist policies of the then-ruling Tokugawa regime. The future leaders of the Meiji era were quietly educated in these schools to favor opening the doors of Japan to Western learning and science.

Miyama's failure to pass the army physical examination led to his eventually sailing to America. There his dream of remaking Japan was turned into remaking the Japanese people with a crusade for Christ, whom he encountered through Dr. Otis Gibson, superintendent of the Chinese Methodist Mission in Chinatown, San Francisco. His meeting with the Lord took place on the evening of February 22, 1877, at about a quarter to nine, in Dr. Gibson's quarters.

Miyama was the first legal immigrant to become a Christian and a minister in America. The actual first Japanese Protestant convert was Joseph Hardy Neejima, usually called Neejima Joe. He had been an illegal stowaway on a voyage to America, according to the laws of Japan. He was baptized in December 31, 1866, at the church of Andover Theological School. Neejima Joe never served a church in America, and later returned to Japan to found Doshisha University in Kyoto.

Eight months after his baptism, Miyama founded the Gospel Society, the first organized group of Japanese in America. He then went on to do the greatest part of the groundwork for the first Japanese church in America, which was finally founded in 1879. The only published reference to this event is found in the 1880 *Journal of the California Conference,* which says, "We recognize the importance of the work initiated among the Japanese, and recommend that our missionaries give it especial care as one that promises large results in the future." It is likely that this church did not become a regular charge until 1884, when Miyama was accepted into the California Conference of the Methodist Episcopal Church and appointed to this Japanese congregation as assistant to Otis Gibson, then supervisor of the Chinese Mission in San Francisco, who supervised the church until he suffered a stroke. Dr. Frederick James Masters succeeded Gibson in 1885 and for the year and a half preceding Harris's arrival in 1866 supervised the church and baptized converts, among them the noted Dr. Takeshi Ukai. In 1885 the California Conference of the Methodist Episcopal Church budgeted $2,100 for this Japanese work, mainly for pastoral support and current expenses.

The first Japanese Methodist church in America had a humble beginning. The small congregation were mostly struggling students and low-paid day laborers. From this small church, though, M. C. Harris and Kanichi Miyama were to expand the Methodist Church's outreach to Japanese in the entire West Coast and eventually into Canada and Hawaii.

Harris took up residence in Oakland and immediately began to minister to the Japanese there and to make frequent trips to San Francisco to oversee Miyama's Japanese church. He also immediately set to work combating the racist persecution of Japanese and Chinese, which had grown to enormous proportions by that time. For this work the California Conference budgeted $4,410 ($1,840 of it for Harris's salary); it also separated Japanese work into its own mission.

From Harris's arrival in 1886 to 1894, Japanese work was in the form of mission stations, first in San Francisco, then in Oakland, then branching out to Sacramento, Portland, Oregon, Fresno, Los Angeles, and many other points. In 1894 Japanese work was organized into a district of the California Conference, along with the Chinese, Norwegian and Danish, and Swedish districts. As a district, it expanded so much that in 1899 Japanese preachers petitioned the General Conference for Mission Conference status; this was granted and remained in effect from 1900 to 1940.

The year of Harris's arrival, Miyama was ordained a deacon. He was admitted to full connection at the 1887 Annual Conference, almost exactly ten years after his dramatic conversion at the hands of Otis Gibson. He was then appointed by the bishop to Japanese mission work in Hawaii. With money collected by his countrymen out of their meager earnings, Kanichi sailed to Honolulu and laid the groundwork for island-wide evangelistic work. He came back to San Francisco once but returned to Hawaii in 1888 and founded the first Japanese Methodist church there, which had thirty-eight members. (This church is now the Harris Memorial Methodist Church.) That year the California Conference budgeted $5,200 for Miyama's Hawaiian Mission work, most of it for his support. During the following Conference year, Miyama baptized 155 persons, among them Ando Taro, the Japanese consul general, and his family; Taro became a zealous and fearless Christian, not only in Hawaii but also in Japan. In 1890 Miyama returned to Japan, where he continued to found churches.

In 1888 the Exclusion Act passed, barring Chinese immigration to the United States. Consequently, Chinese Mission membership growth decreased. However, Japanese Mission membership grew to more than double that of the Chinese in two year's time. Also in this year, the Conference recommended an appropriation of $10,000 for a Japanese mission house. For the Hawaiian Mission a total of $2,000 was appropriated; $5,000 was provided for West Coast work.

By 1887 the Oakland branch mission was growing in numbers and influence. Harris lived in Oakland at 612 15th Street, the site of the Japanese Gospel Society, which had branched out from Miyama's San Francisco Gospel Society, the mother society, in 1886. As in San Francisco, the Japanese Mission used the same site as the Chinese Mission, which was there first, being the older mission.

The Oakland Japanese Methodist Episcopal Church (original name) celebrated its one hundredth anniversary on October 18, 1987, with the Reverend Michael Morizono, one of its lay members turned preacher, as the main speaker. The ceremony gave credit to a Japanese minister as the founder, but that is an error, for there was no Japanese preacher in Oakland at that time. M. C. Harris was the only Japanese-speaking evangelist at that time, and as he had done in Japan, he evangelized the Japanese immigrants as soon as he got there in 1886. Harris was the founder of the Oakland Japanese Methodist Church. Unlike some other missionaries, Harris never lived in a palatial home of his own but lived in rented apartments. Harris lived near and identified with the Japanese people. According to the Oakland church's chronology, its first Japanese pastor, the Reverend Sokichi Doi, did not come until 1889. He started branch missions in 1892 in Berkeley and Alameda, but after he left for San Francisco these branch missions were not kept up for several years. The Alameda branch was restarted by the Methodist Episcopal Church, South, in 1898, and the Berkeley branch did not reopen until about 1908; it was a branch of the Oakland church until 1912; in 1913 it had its first pastor, the Reverend Katahide Yoshioka.

By 1889 there were four mission stations, two in San Francisco, one in Oakland, and one in Los Angeles. The 1889 *Conference Journal* states that these missions were healthy and well organized; in future years the second mission in San Francisco did not survive. In Hawaii there were eight thousand men and one thousand women. The California Conference appropriated $5,000 for a missionary, rent, assistants, and teachers, and $8,000 for the Hawaii Mission for similar expenses. And then for the purpose of securing a mission house, the Conference recommended the appropriation of $10,000 to lay the foundation for Japanese work in Hawaii.

A joyful note in 1889 was the ordination of the second Japanese Methodist minister, Terujiro Hasegawa. So for the first time, with two Japanese ministers and one white superintendent, primarily Japanese pastors ministered to the growing numbers of Japanese in California. Membership climbed from 90 to 165 to 250 by 1889. In 1892 the San Francisco Japanese Mission was the third largest Methodist church with 445 members, the largest being the Central Methodist Church with 620 members. Grace Methodist Church had 487 members.

In 1891 the Japanese ministers on trial were F. Matsuda, T. Shimizu, Sokichi Doi, Terujiro Hasegawa, Jiro Hirota, Teikichi Matsuda, and Teikichi Sunamoto. So superintendent Harris had a good corps of Japanese ministers.

These ministers were all from Japan; it was not until the 1930s that English-speaking ministers came on the scene. The very first one, Kanichi Miyama, had already returned to Japan to found the Ginza Church, Tokyo, and the Kamakura Church, besides becoming a great crusader for the temperance movement.

The 1891 report stated that this marked the highest results, spiritually, in the history of the mission. Since the great revival, which began two years previously, conversions had occurred in ever-increasing numbers. Sixty-five were received into the church, making a total membership of 200, besides 70 probationers. In June 1891 another mission branch, Mount Olivet, was opened in San Francisco, with the Reverend T. Shimizu in charge.

In 1890 the Honolulu District had the following appointments: Ewa, supplied by S. Kobayakawa; Honolulu, Tetsujiro Hasegawa; Kohala, supplied by P. Y. Kaburangi; Koloa, Teikichi Sunamoto; Maui, I. Takatori; Oahu, supplied by K. Wada; Oahu Circuit, supplied by S. Hayashi; Waimea, supplied by K. Suda; Makiki, supplied by K. Wada. In subsequent years many other places were added to the list, such as Lahaina, Hilo, Kaneohe, Kahuku, Waipio, Kula and Hana, some of which are still active (1987).

In late 1890 the California Conference offered the Japanese Methodist Mission to the Hawaiian Board of the Congregational Church, and in December 1891 it withdrew. However, three ministers remained, two of them being probationers, because the need was so great. The Japanese Methodists in Hawaii made strong petition for the resumption of Methodist work, so it was reopened in 1893, but some damage had been done, and some members had been lost. The Reverend Kikutaro Matsuno was the first to return as an official appointee, followed by T. Takahashi. It was deemed a big mistake to have withdrawn from the work even temporarily.

The 1892 report stated that Japanese brethren had gone everywhere preaching the gospel—to public assemblies, highways, byways, the hospitals, prisons, clubs, lodging houses, ranches, and gambling houses. Three thousand tracts were distributed. The Oakland church opened two new branches in Berkeley and Alameda, as stated elsewhere. The Sacramento branch received its first full minister, in Hokashichi Kihara, in February 1892, embracing Sacramento, Vacaville, Winters, and the valley. One hundred sixteen were converted, and thirty were baptized.

The 1892 report also speaks of a blessed harvest. The result for the year 1892 of the revival that began in 1889 was 600 conversions and 250 adults and one child baptized.

In the Conference of 1893 Bishop Edward G. Andrews ordained as deacons Zenro Hirota, Teikichi Sunamoto, and Kikutaro Matsuno. Admitted into full membership were Sokichi Doi, Tetsujiro Hasegawa, and Zenro Hirota.

There was continuous revival at nearly all stations. The laborers reported that over 1,000 persons converted, and 850 had been baptized. In October

1892 Teikichi Kawabe visited the Japanese in Oregon, Idaho, and Washington. In January 1893 he returned to Portland, Oregon, and opened a mission, which is planning to celebrate its hundredth anniversary in 1993.

The Hawaii District, which was resuscitated, decided to appropriate money for both Japanese and English work in Honolulu. The total Japanese Mission members were 554, with 300 probationers. The Chinese Mission had 110 members and 25 probationers. (These figures include the West Coast and Hawaii.)

The names of Takeshi Ukai, Tokutaro Nakamura, and Hokashichi Kihara deserve a little mention. Takeshi Ukai was baptized by Frederick James Masters of the Chinese Mission, received his training most likely in the Midwest, became a member of the Des Moines Conference, and transferred into the California Conference. He later became the famous pastor of the Ginza Church in Tokyo. Tokutaro Nakamura transferred in from the Japan Conference. Hokashichi Kihara became an elder and a full member of the Conference and went on to do notable work in Hawaii. In 1894 the Japanese District, which included Hawaii, had a budget of $11,550 and 773 full members and 650 probationers. Over 1,000 of the new conversions came within three years. There were six regular churches and eight branches.

In 1896 the Hawaii District had appropriations for Maui Mission, Honolulu Japanese and Honolulu English work, Waianai, Sprecklesville, Lahaina, and Hana. But some stations did not last too long, mainly due to lack of preachers and money. Three ministers, including Sokichi Doi, who did splendid work in Oakland and San Francisco, returned to Japan to serve in the Japan Methodist Church Conference.

In 1897 the Honolulu Mission reported 217 conversions the past year. On the West Coast churches in Los Angeles, Fresno, Watsonville, Sacramento, Oakland, Vacaville, San Francisco, and Portland increased their memberships daily. All told, over two hundred adults were baptized, and five hundred were converted. In the mid-1890s the names of Morizo Yoshida and Zenro Hirota became prominent. Morizo Yoshida went on to serve several churches until he passed away in 1919. Zenro Hirota served for decades into the 1930s, when he retired.

Watsonville, California, was a Methodist mission with regularly appointed ministers from 1897 to 1900, but in an ecumenical agreement with the Presbyterians it was given over to them. It is now called Westview Presbyterian Church. Since then Methodists have not entered the Salinas-Watsonville area among the Japanese.

On September 11, 1899, the members of the Pacific Japanese District petitioned the General Conference, which met in 1900, to organize the Japanese churches into a Mission Conference to further enhance the work among the increasing number of Japanese immigrants in both Hawaii and the mainland. They felt that all interests of the Japanese work would be enhanced thereby. With the passing of the enabling act of the 1900 General Conference, Bishop John W. Hamilton announced the Pacific organization of the Japanese Methodist Episcopal Mission. Admitted into full membership were Tokusaburo Morimoto and Yoshisuke Sacon. Taihei Takahashi and Genshichi Tsuruda were ordained deacons, and Morizo Yoshida was ordained elder, all by Bishop Hamilton.

In 1901 the Japanese Mission Conference was divided into a Hawaii District and a Pacific Coast District. In the Hawaii District the appointments were for Honolulu English, Honolulu Japanese, Aiea and Waipahu, Hana Circuit, Kona, Kula, Lahaina. G. L. Pearson was the presiding elder. In the Pacific Coast District the presiding elder was M. C. Harris. Individual charges were Fresno, Los Angeles, Oakland, Pocatello, Idaho, Portland, Riverside, Sacramento, San Francisco, San Jose, and Vacaville. Two ministers were transferred back to Japan. Zenro Hirota and Suenoshin Kawashima left without appointment to attend school; they both came back eventually to serve long, fruitful ministries at many churches. Normally Japanese ministers had their seminary education in Japan and then took some seminary education in the United States, so they were pretty well educated.

A description of the Aiea-Waipahu charge is very revealing. Brother Taihei Takahashi visited the four camps regularly every week, looked after the sick, conducted a night school, and preached. Mrs. Takahashi accompanied him to assist in the work. At Aiea a Japanese day school was taught by Mrs. Takahashi, with 20 pupils attending. Mrs. Takahashi was also superintendent of the Sunday school. A night school, prayer services, and public worship were conducted regularly at Aiea with great results in the physical and moral transformation of the people. This shows the type of pioneer work that the early preachers undertook, and that the wife of the minister did just as much work or more.

The 1901 report states that the Japanese Mission churches were made into a district of the California Conference by Bishop Andrews in September 1893, and M. C. Harris was appointed presiding elder. So for seven years all of Hawaii and the West Coast was one separate district. Membership grew every year, even though there were many losses due to the constant movement of immigrants from place to place. In 1892 there were 445 members, and 450 probationers. In 1894, a banner year, it went as high as 733, then it went down a little, and in 1900 membership was 627 and 338 probationers. In 1901 there were 627 members; in 1902, 755 members; in 1904, 904 members and 710 probationers (figures for 1903 not available). So the Japanese churches as a district and as an autonomous mission Conference, under M. C. Harris, had grown over 100 percent.

M. C. Harris was superintendent until the General Conference of 1904, when he was elected bishop of Japan and Korea. When the Japanese Mission Conference was held from August 31 to September 5 of 1904 at San

Francisco, Dr. Herbert Buell Johnson, a returned missionary from Japan, was already the presiding elder or superintendent. Due to travel delays and illness in his family, the new superintendent could not do as much work as he desired. However, he did visit six of the churches before the Annual Conference. Most of the groundwork was done by M. C. Harris for two-thirds of the year, so we give Harris credit through 1904.

By 1903 he had mission churches in San Francisco, Oakland, Sacramento, Vacaville, Portland, Seattle, Tacoma, Spokane, Victoria, Vancouver, Fraser River, and Union in British Columbia; also Fresno, San Jose, Los Angeles, Riverside, and Watsonville. In later years the British Columbia charges and Watsonvile discontinued as Pacific Japanese Mission charges or churches.

In 1904 appointments were made to Fresno and Selma, Los Angeles, Oakland, Oxnard, Pocatella, Idaho, Portland, Riverside, Sacramento, San Francisco, San Jose, Seattle, and Anglo-Japanese Training School. These appointments were for the Pacific Coast District. For the Hawaii Mission appointments were to Aiea and Pearl City, Hana, Honolulu English, Honolulu Japanese, South King Street, Kaanapali, Kapaa and Kealia, Kahuku and Waianae, Korean Mission, Lahaina, and Waipahu.

Under Harris churches were extended from Los Angeles and Riverside in Southern California to British Columbia in Canada; to Pocatello, Idaho; to Oahu, Maui, and the other Hawaiian islands; and to most of Northern California. Succeeding superintendents were to establish churches in more communities, as well as to extend into the Denver, Colorado area.

THE ANGLO-JAPANESE TRAINING SCHOOL

A special word should be said about the Anglo-Japanese Training School, which was begun under the supervision of M. C. Harris. It became a full-time school with professional teachers and hundreds of students every year. The aim of the school was to teach English as well as Christianity.

In the 1901 *California Conference Journal* report it says six young men completed the three-year course and graduated in June 1901. That would mean that the school began at least by 1898. The enrollment for 1901 was 200, and the average attendance was 140 per month. It was mainly an English language school to fit pupils for schools in America but it also taught conversational English, mainly to new arrivals. The Reverend Yoshisuke Sacon, later professor of Hebrew in Aoyama Gakuin Seminary, was the principal in 1901.

In 1902 the Reverend Zenro Hirota was the principal of the school in the list of appointments, but in the superintendent's report it says Pastor Kyugoro Obata conducted the school after Principal Y. Sacon left. In the appointment list Dr. Milton S. Vail is listed as a teacher in the Anglo-Japanese Training

School, but from 1904 on Dr. Vail was the principal. Vail, a distinguished educator who for twenty years was prominently connected with the Methodist educational work in Japan, was the son of Dr. Stephen M. Vail, one of the founders of the first Methodist theological school in America. He knew Daniel Drew and Mrs. Eliza Garrett, names connected with the founding of Drew Theological Seminary and Garrett Biblical Institute. Stephen Vail sent his youngest son, Milton, to train young men in Japan, and by the 1900s he was training young Japanese immigrants in America.

Under him, with the encouragement of Superintendent H. B. Johnson, a Bible training class was organized in the school in 1904 to give preliminary training for future evangelists. In 1906, even after the earthquake, they had four students in the theological department, eight teachers, and an enrollment of pupils. Seven young men were graduated. In 1907 four hundred pupils were enrolled. There were four white and five Japanese teachers, all thoroughly trained.

The 1909 school year had seven teachers and two sessions of schoolwork, one in the afternoon and one in the evening. The morning session had too few registrants, so it was given up. Ten young men graduated, some entering high schools and others going to the Methodist colleges in California. The enrollment for seven years is given thus: 1903—291 pupils; 1904—299; 1905—300; 1906—380; 1907—330; 1908—356; 1909—231. The drop in the 1909 enrollment was due to emigration laws of Japan, hard times, and the moving of the school six blocks from the center of Japanese population. Due to lack of school funds, a $1.50 per month tuition fee had to be charged, a large sum for families at a time when most of them earned from $3 to $5 a week. The theological education class had difficulty in being kept up for various reasons.

In 1910 enrollment went down to 141, 133 men and 8 women. In 1909 there were nine graduates, three of them women. The majority of the men entered high schools in San Francisco. In 1911 enrollment was 178, 13 of whom were women. Four were graduated to enter high school. There were eight teachers in the San Francisco school and three in Oakland. In 1912 there were 170 enrolled, 12 of whom were women. There were five teachers in the day school and four in the night school.

In the tenth year of Dr. Vail's principalship, 1913, the school was fifteen years old. This school was said to be the only school of high order for Japanese in America, and it was well and favorably known up and down the Pacific Coast. Baron Chinda, ambassador then at Washington, D.C., the Christian diplomat Kawakami, and Yonezawa, general superintendent of railways in Manchuria, were all graduates of this school. First-, second-, third-, and fourth-year classes and 6 postgraduates made a total of 160 enrolled, 19 of whom were women. In 1914 2 graduated.

In 1915 there were 178 enrolled, with 32 women. There were 8 graduates at this 22nd commencement. This was the year of World War I.

The fall term had 117 enrolled, 14 of them women, and 2 graduates. Five were baptized. The spring term had 162 enrolled, 25 of them women; there were 8 graduates, 1 a woman.

In 1918 spring term there were 156 enrolled, with 21 women. The fall term had 159 enrolled, with 20 women. Three graduated. This year Dr. John L. Hatfield, one of the teachers, bought and donated the property next to the San Francisco church, to be used for the Anglo-Japanese Training School.

In 1924 the U.S. Congress passed the infamous Oriental Exclusion Law, aimed at the Japanese. The Methodist General Conference sent a strongly worded resolution to the U.S. Congress opposing this law, and Dr. H. B. Johnson spoke far and wide against it, but to no avail. The law excluding Japanese immigration was passed, thus severely wounding a proud nation.

For the Anglo-Japanese School, it began to decrease in enrollment from 1924 on. In 1925 there were fewer than one hundred pupils. In 1926 average attendance was only nine pupils. In 1927 total enrollment was nineteen. The Exclusion Act had almost totally cut off the entry of the type of Japanese formerly served by this school. The last report of the Anglo-Japanese Training School to the Annual Conference of the Pacific Japanese Mission was made in 1927.

Thus ended a very notable school for Japanese immigrants. For thirty-three years, it did a splendid service to the Pacific Japanese Mission Conference.

THE PERIOD OF THE SECOND SUPERINTENDENT, HERBERT BUELL JOHNSON

Dr. Herbert Buell Johnson was born April 30, 1858, in New York. He was converted in 1876. After graduating from Drew Seminary, he married in New York in 1883 and then served several pastorates in the Wyoming Conference (New York). He sailed from San Francisco for Japan on November 18, 1887, where he served as a missionary until 1904, the year he succeeded M. C. Harris as superintendent of the Pacific Japanese Mission. For the next twenty-one years he threw himself into Christian work with the Japanese in a manner that built up a strong and vital Japanese Methodist Episcopal Church on the Pacific Coast.

More than any other man on the Coast, he helped to clarify and stabilize the thinking of the Christian people on the Japanese question. At a time when the Japanese and Japanese Americans had no voice to defend themselves because the second-generation Japanese Americans (Nisei) were just children and the immigrants were at the mercy of demagogues, H. B. Johnson was like a voice in the wilderness crying out vigorously against injustice, especially against the 1924 Immigration Exclusion Act. He was mercilessly accused of being a "Jap lover," yet he led the General Conference of the Methodist Episcopal Church to send a strong resolution to President Coolidge to veto the Oriental

Exclusion law. All his struggles against racial prejudice broke his health, and he finally succumbed to a heart attack on a train in North Platte, Nebraska. The local Methodist pastor took him to the hospital where he passed away. Bishop Burns at the Board of Home Missions and Church Extension meeting said of him, "In this generation Dr. Johnson is the outstanding Christian statesman on the Pacific Coast. No other man has made a more significant contribution to racial understanding in terms of religious expression than he. He is our Methodist ambassador extraordinary to the Japanese." The Emperor of Japan, some years before, as in the case of M. C. Harris, had given him the highest decoration given to a foreigner.

Johnson vigorously promoted the growth of the churches founded by M. C. Harris and Kanichi Miyama and went beyond into other communities and territories. The Seattle church, which just started in the time of M. C. Harris, became firmly established; the Tacoma church was founded in 1908, Oxnard in 1905, and Bakersfield in 1906. Palo Alto in 1910 had a separate appropriation but actually got started by Katahide Yoshioka in 1908 and 1909. Loomis, cared for by the Sacramento pastor for some time, had its separate establishment in 1911, although it was still supplied from Sacramento until the Reverend Y. Naito came in 1913. Berkeley, which had services from 1892 to 1894 but lost its appropriation for several years, finally received its first separate funding in 1912. The Berkeley church united with the Japanese Christian Church in 1929, and it is still a united church but completely Methodist administered. The Florin church was opened by the Reverend Yasaburo Tsuda in 1913 but merged with the Sacramento church to become the Sacramento Japanese United Methodist Church in 1968. H. B. Johnson began work in Brawley in 1913 and in 1920 secured a good corner lot and built a splendid church there. Brawley was one of the churches that had to be sold after World War II because not enough people returned after the evacuation. The venerable Kosaburo Baba served first in 1913, I. Nishimura from 1914 to 1916, S. Takata in 1917, H. Arima from 1919 to 1923, S. Arima from 1924 to 1925, and S. Miyazaki in 1926. From 1927 to 1932 the Reverend Chozo Haruyama served Brawley, followed by Susumu Kuwano, a layman turned preacher.

Another new field opened by H. B. Johnson was in Colorado and Nebraska. H. Shigeta opened both the Pueblo and the Denver churches. The Pueblo circuit extended into the Arkansas Valley; the Denver circuit covered the South Platte Valley. The West Nebraska circuit, which covered the North Platte Valley, with Scottsbluff as its center, was served by S. Saito for two years. Reno, Nevada, Missoula, Montana, and Stockton, California, were preaching circuits for periods of two years or more. Except for Denver, which became one of the biggest churches, the other points in the mountain area and Stockton are no longer served.

Some young ministers who were prominent during Johnson's time were

Morizo Yoshida, Oto So, Yasaburo Tsuda, Yuzuru Yamaka, Tokuji Komuro, and Iwakichi Haratani. Zenro Hirota and Suenoshin Kawashima were older ministers who served either Hawaii or the West Coast till their very end. The newer ministers were Chozo Haruyama, T. J. Machida, and Mrs. Aya Okuda, the only woman preacher, who served many years in the former Japanese Conference. She served for fifteen years before she died in an automobile accident.

During H. B. Johnson's time the geographical extension of Japanese work was at its widest, going as far inland as Nebraska, even at a time of extreme racial prejudice. Johnson had to spend considerable time fighting for Japanese rights and lost his life doing it. Also, the problem of bilingual and English work gradually began to be prominent.

The founding of two other churches should be credited to Dr. Johnson: Bakersfield founded in 1906 with the help of the Reverend K. Nagasaki from Fresno, and Loomis, established as a separate charge in 1911. Bakersfield has changed its name in recent years to St. Andrew's United Methodist Church; it is mostly pastored by a neighboring white pastor, but the Japanese-speaking group in the congregation has been cared by the Reverend Alpha H. Takagi, retired, who drives in from San Gabriel. Loomis church has been for many years now a predominantly white church with white pastors. However, it keeps its ties with Japanese circles through the Sacramento districts of both the Methodists and the Japanese Church Federation.

Dr. H. B. Johnson increased the total Japanese membership from 923 to 1672, Sunday school enrollment from 1951 to 2460, and ministerial support from $6,925 to $14,127 during his twenty-one years of superintendency. He had a wider vision of increasing work in Fresno, Sacramento Valley, Santa Clara Valley, Imperial Valley, Denver and Northern Colorado, and Pueblo and Southern Colorado, but he passed away before he could accomplish anything in those areas.

CONTRIBUTIONS OF THE PARENT METHODIST BODIES

The boards of foreign mission of the Methodist Episcopal Church and the Methodist Episcopal Church, South, and Methodist Episcopal Church Women's Foreign Missionary Society, and the Women's Home Missionary Society all sent missionaries to Japan, and in the case of the Home Missionary Society sent missionaries to work among the Japanese on the West Coast and Hawaii. These missionaries were a source of leadership, especially as superintendents of the Pacific Japanese Mission. The first was M. C. Harris (1886–1904), followed by Herbert Buell Johnson (1904–1925), Frank Herron Smith (1926–1945), and John B. Cobb (1945–1946).

The Women's Foreign Missionary Society sent many women missionaries to various places. Some were from the Methodist Episcopal Church, South, but when they returned about 1941 and 1942, they were all part of the Methodist Church. In 1941 Miss Azalea Peat was helping at Portland, Oregon. Miss Anna Bell Williams was at Lodi, California. By 1945 the following were assigned to help the Japanese in any way they could: C. Holland, Denver, Colorado; M. Searcy, Greeley, Colorado; Doris Wagner, Blanca, Colorado; E. Hempstead, Twin Falls, Idaho; C. Teague, Idaho Falls, Idaho; Azalea Peat, Nyssa, Oregon; Alice Finley, Ontario, Oregon. In 1946 the following missionaries were utilized: Alice Cheney, Seattle, Washington; Bertha Starkey, Reedley, California; Alice Peavy, Los Angeles, California; Doris Wagner, Pueblo, Colorado; C. Stevens, Dinuba, California. In 1947 Alice Finly helped at Wapato, Washington, and Anna Bell Williams at Walnut Grove, California.

Some of the men who assisted were as follows: the Reverend S. A. Stewart supplied Mesa, Arizona, for several years; Dr. H. Victor Martin helped in Denver and Palo Alto for several years; Dr. Frederick W. Heckelman took care of the El Monte Church in Los Angeles for some years; Dr. John B. Cobb supplied the Spokane Church during the war years; I. L. Shaver was at Caldwell, Idaho, and assisted the Minidoka Camp ministry. A nonmissionary lay preacher, Fred Fertig, assisted in Berkeley, Mt. View, and Los Angeles up to 1949. Other young whites helped at various local churches as English assistants. Then there were many local laywomen who worked hard in building the Japanese churches by taking care of the Sunday schools and some young peoples' work, as in Spokane, Seattle, Palo Alto, Mt. View, San Jose, Portland, Bakersfield, Wapato, and other churches.

The Women's Home Missionary Society built substantial homes in Honolulu, San Francisco, Seattle, and Los Angeles. As early as 1903 the Susannah Wesley Home in Honolulu was open for women and children. In 1924 a larger home was dedicated for this school.

The Ellen Stark Ford Home at 2025 Pine Street, San Francisco, had 32 people, twelve of them under age five, in 1911. A kindergarten with 30 children was conducted. Japanese and Korean languages were taught in the afternoons. Including three teachers, there were six workers in the home.

In 1911 in Seattle, at 11th and Terrace, a house was purchased and named the Catherine J. Elaine Home. A superintendent and a Japanese worker were staff people. It became a home for women and girls. From the 1920s to the 1940s the home was also a residence for youth ministers and youth women workers, such as the Reverend Lester Suzuki (1946–1948), Edith Tsuruda (1930), and Iseko Hayakawa (1932). It was also a hostel in the postwar period.

The Jane Couch Home, Los Angeles, was first located on Arlington Street. In the 1910s and 1920s it was at 1350 South Burlington Street, and in the 1930s it was at 1224 West 35th Street, where the English pastor resided. In 1911 forty women and seven children stayed there for varying amounts of time. In 1912 twelve women and five children were cared for. Morning worship was in English; in the evening it was conducted in Japanese. In 1915

Mrs. Kataoka, a deaconness, was secured, and she served for some years.

The Susannah Wesley Home in Honolulu, the Catherine Blaine Home in Seattle, and the Ellen Stark Ford Home in San Francisco respectively report figures of forty, fifty, and sixty women and children cared for; they also established kindergartens and secured Japanese deaconesses to work with the women and children and conduct Bible classes. In 1917 the Ellen Stark Ford Home reported that seventy-two children and forty-seven women passed through the home. Their cumulative totals up to that year were 11,874 persons, staying for a day and a night, and 3,565,100 meals served. Girls who stayed at the home finished high school, and some went on to college.

In San Jose there was no home, but the Women's Home Missionary Society opened a kindergarten in 1918 with fifteen enrolled, which was made possible through a donation by D. C. Crummey.

Unlike the Anglo-Japanese Training School, which died due to the Oriental Exclusion Law of 1924, these homes for women and children remained open because they served American-born women and children, not immigrants. However, gradually the homes' reports to the Annual Conference diminished in size and detail. What used to be work of great significance was gradually phased out.

One great result of the women's work was the inspiration given to the American-born Nisei women, who responded to Dr. Frank Herron Smith's Macedonian call, proclaimed in 1926 at a massive Young Peoples' Christian Conference, to Dr. Herron's challenge, "We need 500 Nisei preachers and religious workers to minister to the entire Japanese population." The women were the first to respond. Already Margaret Tann (later Uyei) had entered the field, in 1924 and 1925. Others followed—Edith Tsuruda (Furuki), Dorothy Funabiki, Yuki Kuwahara, Mary Oyama, Sumile Morishita, Rose Naka, Iseko Hayakaway, Grace Takahashi (who served Wapato Church in 1933 and 1934), Doris Aiso, and Mariyo Okazaki (who served Los Angeles in 1939 and Kingsburg in 1940). These women were ahead of the men, who started coming in from 1933 on. Because women were not accepted in the ministry, most of them served short years. One white woman, Helen May Smith, served as deaconess and youth worker in Seattle and Denver in the late 1940s and early 1950s and then went on to serve in the San Pedro Toberman Settlement House. She was sponsored by the Women's Home Missionary Society.

THE PERIOD OF THE THIRD SUPERINTENDENT, DR. FRANK HERRON SMITH

After the death of Herbert Buell Smith, the bishop appointed Dr. Frank Herron Smith as superintendent, in July 1926. Smith left Kansas to be a missionary to Japan, where he served for twenty-two years. He, like his missionary predecessors, spoke Japanese fluently and was a popular speaker before Young Peoples' Christian Conferences in Japan.

Before the economic crash of 1929, Dr. Smith enjoyed three good years, and by 1928 he had added Wapato, Hood River, Salem, Oregon, and Marysville. Branch work was started in Delano from Bakersfield by the Reverend Yasuo Oshita. The Reverend Chozo Haruyama made trips to Arizona from Brawley to begin some new work there.

As emphasis was given to English-speaking ministers, Japanese American ministers began to come in: Masaichi Goto (first Nisei), Shigeo Tanabe, Lester E. Suzuki, Hideo Hashimoto, Waichi Cyanagi, Paul Hagiya, Norio Yasaki, Samuel Takagishi, and Masagi Goto. And then young ministers with Japanese training came in, before World War II: Caspar Horikoshi, Andrew Kuroda, J. K. Sasaki, Taro Goto, and Shigeo Shimada.

Then came the stock market crash of 1929. Dr. Smith's superintendency thus coincided with the Great Depression and then World War II, with all its trials and tribulations. In spite of the Depression, younger Nisei ministers came in to begin at incredibly low salaries. During the 1930s Board of Missions support became less and less every year, and Dr. Smith was told to eliminate some ministers to meet the budget, but instead he chose to cut out aid across the board, so all would share in the suffering. Dr. Smith led a very frugal life, never staying in high-priced hotels. In spite of his having polio, he vigorously made his rounds of quarterly Conferences and preachings, conducted in both English and Japanese.

During this time the unification of the Methodist churches took place, so to his administration were added the five Methodist Episcopal Church, South, churches of Alameda, Oakland, Walnut Grove, Dinuba, and Sonoma County. Of these, Oakland and Sonoma County eventually disappeared. Oakland members were invited to the Methodist Episcopal Oakland church, which today is the Lake Park United Methodist Church. The Methodist Episcopal Church, South had started with the Alameda church in 1892, and Superintendent W. A. Davis was also a Japanese-speaking missionary.

In 1929 Livingston was added to Dr. Smith's charge. It was at first an independent church; the Reverend Sozaburo Watanabe was appointed there. In 1931 West Los Angeles was added. In 1932 Mesa, Arizona, was added, with Aya Okuda as its supply pastor. In 1929 Santa Maria, led by the Reverend Y. Oshita, came into the Methodist Conference. It was a union church with the Presbyterian and Congregational churches involved. El Monte, under the Reverend Jutaro Yokoi, came in 1934.

The Reverend Shigeo Tanabe was a first Nisei minister when he began in Spokane in 1933, and he was first Nisei at San Francisco and Sacramento. Lester E. Suzuki was a first Nisei minister in Wapato (1935), Los Angeles, and Seattle. Others followed in the 1930s, 1940s, and 1950s, but today's ministers are mostly third generation (Sansei) or Japan-trained ministers, and a few whites. In 1987 among active ministers, there were only two Nisei left, so a new generation has taken control.

When Dr. F. H. Smith assumed his post in 1926, there were twenty-one Japanese churches. There were thirty-two in 1938, and after unification there were thirty-seven. For some years after the war, the Chicago Fellowship Church and the Seabrook, New Jersey, churches were administered by the Japanese Conference, making the total thirty-nine. Only the New York Japanese church was not under the Pacific Japanese Provisional Conference.

When World II came, the unconstitutional evacuation of all people of Japanese descent, defined as having up to one-sixteenth Japanese blood, took place in the spring of 1942. The people evacuated were from the war zones of California, Oregon, Washington, and the southern portion of Arizona. The only Methodist churches not evacuated were the Spokane and Denver churches. Most of the Mesa church was evacuated. So immediately Japanese Methodists could not meet as a Conference in a normal way. The 1942 Annual Conference was held in the Santa Anita Assembly Center, with military guards posted at all doors. Even the bishop, James Chamberlain Baker, was escorted there by armed soldiers. With the business hurriedly administered, all the appointments were to the military zone, wherever ministers were incarcerated.

In every camp, in the fifteen assembly centers, and in the ten so-called relocation centers (which were actually concentration camps, complete with barbed wire, armed watch towers, military units watching), there were Methodists. The preachers immediately went to work to organize Sunday schools, worship services, Bible studies, prayer meetings, young people's meetings, and even big conferences within the camps. In the main it was interdenominational work, where all cooperated except for a few who chose not to cooperate.

Quite often white preachers were invited in to preach and give workshops. The National Council of Churches sponsored some Great Preaching Missions in many camps, where national leaders such as Earl Stanley Jones took the lead. They were quite successful. And then for a few Christmas seasons, churches, Sunday schools, and women's groups throughout the nation sent Christmas gifts so that all children in every camp could receive Christmas gifts from some unknown person. Those were the few bright memories of those infamous camps.

Superintendent Smith, along with all other denomination heads, organized a Wartime Commission for Japanese Service, trying to improve conditions in the camps and becoming a liaison with the Army and the administration. Ministers could not be paid the $19 a month government pay due to the Constitutional separation of church and state, so the Protestant Commission paid all the ministers, including the Japanese Salvation Army officers, who were abandoned by the parent Salvation Army. With all the good the Salvation Army does, their sad treatment of the Japanese Salvation Army Corps was really un-Christian.

Smith was maligned and abused as a "Jap-Lover," like his predecessor H. B. Johnson. Insurance companies often dropped the insurance of Japanese churches; Dr. Smith mortgaged his house to pay for some of the dropped insurances. He endured so much stress that he finally succumbed to a heart attack at the Cheyenne, Wyoming, train station. He expected to die, but his prayer to God was a promise, that if he lived he would preserve intact all the Japanese churches so they could go back to them after the war, while the church at large was advocating abandoning ethnic churches as such. That was the wisest thing, because every church became a postwar hostel for many families and individuals, until they could find homes and jobs.

Those were trying days. Because of Dr. Smith's foresight, all the Methodist churches remained intact except for two churches, Brawley and Vacaville, which had to be sold. Today most all the churches are well, and they owe a debt of gratitude to Frank Herron Smith for his wise policy, enforced in spite of opposition.

During Dr. Smith's time, due to government encouragement, some ministers and many lay people went out of the camps to try their luck in the Midwest and East. The Reverend Shigeo Tanabe went to New York; Lester Suzuki went to Des Moines for hostel work; Yonosuke Sasaki went to Seabrook, New Jersey; Andrew Kuroda went to Washington, D.C.; Casper Horikoshi went to Boston; Katahide Yoshioka went to Chicago; and T. J. Machida went to Washington, D.C., to teach in a language school. Most of them came back eventually, but some few never came back.

THE POSTWAR PERIOD AND THE TARO GOTO PERIOD

For a brief period in 1945 and early 1946, due to the sickness of Frank Herron Smith, Dr. John B. Cobb, Sr., who ministered the Spokane church during the war, became interim superintendent. He also took care of the Alameda church until a minister could be appointed in 1946. Dr. Cobb had been a Southern Methodist missionary to Japan most of his life, so it was real relief to Smith to have somebody who was able to do the same type of work among Japanese churches.

Then in 1946 Dr. Channing A. Richardson, not a missionary but a prominent pastor, was chosen as superintendent. He served for three years, during a trying time of the reorganizing and regrouping of the former churches. Already by 1948, through an enabling act of the General Conference, the Western Jurisdiction was empowered to invite Japanese churches, and the Colorado Conference had already sent a request. So the matter of integration into the general church had already officially started. Of course at that time the Japanese Provisional Annual Conference was only eight years old, so integration was not their desire. Serious discussion of that was to come much later.

At the Western Jurisdiction Conference of July 1948, three new bishops were elected, one of whom was Donald Harvey Tippett. He chose the Reverend Taro Goto to become the first and only Japanese superintendent of the Japanese Provisional Annual Conference. Goto was superintendent from 1949 to 1964, the year of the merger.

The system of assistant district superintendents, begun in Channing Richardson's time, was utilized. Assistant superintendents were appointed in the Pacific Northwest, Northwest Inland, Central California, San Francisco Bay, Southwest, and Colorado Conferences. Samuel Takagishi started in Los Angeles in 1947 but died an untimely death while still young. Paul Hagiya (1947), Lloyd Wake (1949), and Arnold Nakajima (1951) were all stationed in Berkeley as student pastors. Kiyoshi Nagai did supply work in Bakersfield (1949), Oakland (1951), and Loomis (1950). Roy Sano supplied at Oxnard in 1950, and Lloyd Wake started full-time at San Francisco in 1950. Lester E. Suzuki came to Berkeley in 1952 for a long pastorate. Casper Horikoshi came to Oakland in 1953. John H. Yamashita had done a very good job of reopening Oakland in 1945 and served till 1952, when he was appointed to Los Angeles. Alpha Takagi assisted in El Monte in 1950 and made a good record in several churches, the last being Palo Alto. Harry Murakami got his start in Sacramento in 1952 and Wesley Yamaka at Oakland in 1950. Harper Sakaue came from the Baptist Church to start at Fresno in 1952. Except for such older men as Lester Suzuki and Casper Horikoshi, the rest were younger men or seminary graduates who were brought in during Taro Goto's superintendency. Joseph Sakakibara was on trial in 1953 but he did not take an appointment until 1957, when he was assigned to Dinuba.

George Uyemura was an effective minister, starting as Denver's assistant pastor in 1947. He took over the Fresno church in 1949. George Nishikawa started in Sacramento in 1948; he later served as district superintendent in the Pacific Southwest Conference. Peter Chen started at Riverside in 1957 and later served in the Board of Discipleship, as well as at Centenary and San Jose churches. Sadao Masuko started in Ontario, Oregon, in 1947. Michael Morizono, a lay state of California worker called to the ministry, started in 1961 as Oakland's assistant and had a successful career at Wesley San Jose and as Fresno district superintendent in the Cal-Nevada Conference.

Beginning in the mid-1950s the English-speaking Nisei were the appointed pastors, and the Issei (first generation Japanese born in the United States) ministers became the assistants, reversing the tide of earlier years. Examples in 1956 were Jiryu Fujii at Berkeley, T. J. Machida at Los Angeles, Susumu Kuwano at Sacramento, Iwakichi Haratani at San Francisco, Yasuo Oshita at Santa Maria, and Juhei C. Kono at Seattle. This pattern was kept up for many years. However, in the 1970s and 1980s the Japanese-speaking divisions have become so small that a full ministry had become difficult to administer. Only a few large churches at Seattle, San Jose, Los Angeles, Denver, and West Los Angeles have full-time language ministers. Smaller churches have guest preachers or shared ministry on a part-time basis. This in spite of the fact that thousands of new Japanese immigrants or arrivals are in our midst waiting to be ministered to.

A few churches have changed in substance due to change in emphasis. The Oxnard church merged with a white church and for all practical purposes promptly disappeared. The Japanese-speaking group had guest ministers as long as they could, but that too is about gone. The Loomis church became the First Methodist Church and opened its doors to all comers, and the white newcomers so outnumbered the Japanese that it is now no longer considered a Japanese church. The minister is always white. When the Livingston church merged with the First Methodist Church, the Japanese members again became the stronger element, and they now control the church. The same is true of the Lake Park Church in Oakland, formerly purely Japanese. It merged with what was basically a Norwegian- and Swedish-descent church, and whites are practically not there anymore.

Some positive things that the Provisional Conference, as an independent and autonomous Conference, could do and did was to plan their own Conference Evangelism program. Emphasis was placed in certain areas, such as Central California or the Gardena area, the Northwest area, and so on. The Conference was able to send delegates to many national and regional conferences such as were held by the Council on Evangelism, the Regional Conference of the Board of Missions, the Convocation on Christian Social Concerns, the Western Jurisdictional School of the Women's Society of Christian Service, and the Western Jurisdictional Conference Officers meeting. The Conference organized a Pastors' School for many years, geared to Japanese pastors' specific needs. For the Women's Society of Christian Service the members had a Conference-wide gathering every year, and other district gatherings, covering the entire Western Jurisdiction. Members of the society often talk about these gatherings with nostalgia. After the churches became small parts of each larger Annual Conference, such gatherings were not possible. District lay conferences were enjoyable events. The Japanese-language divisions really enjoyed their occasional Conference-wide and district-wide gatherings, and even after the Japanese Conference was no longer in existence, they kept up the district gatherings, for they were never a part of the larger Conference in spirit and language.

The movement for integration of Japanese churches began when the General Conference in 1948 enabled Conferences to invite a Japanese church away from its own Provisional Conference. The first such invitation was issued by the Colorado Conference. Although their move was defeated thirty-eight to two, the movement for integration was being promoted behind the scenes.

Annual Conferences were encouraged to invite Japanese pastors as guests. The Board of Pensions was making plans ahead of time to take care of pension matters such as which Conference would pay what portion and other details. The bishop and superintendent stated their neutrality on the subject of integration, but it turned out that they were silently encouraging the process. A target date of 1964 was set, but great concerns and apprehension were felt by the Japanese as the time drew near. They wanted and yet did not want to be merged. It was not a one-sided feeling.

In the postwar period the English-speaking leadership took control. Tremendous building projects were undertaken: eleven new sanctuaries were constructed, two sanctuaries were purchased, thirteen new educational buildings were constructed, and nineteen parsonages were purchased, so there was tremendous growth. All this action was reminiscent of the very early years when Japanese preachers and evangelists, encouraged by M. C. Harris, went about preaching everywhere. But this drive was to lose quite a bit of steam when the Japanese churches became minor segments of four Annual Conferences. Up until integration the Japanese conferences had control of entire Western states and were empowered to expand and evangelize on their own power.

At the final Conference held on May 23, 1964, at San Francisco, the appointments took the form of transfers. To Rocky Mountain Conference went Jonathan Fujita and Paul Hagiya; to Pacific Northwest went Juhei C. Kono, Harry Murakami, Shigeo Shimada, Wesley Yamaka, and Robert Yamashita; to Oregon Annual Conference went Waichi Oyanagi; to Idaho Annual Conference went George Uyemura. The following went to the Cal-Nevada Annual Conference: Junichi Fujimori, Masagi Goto, Taro Goto, Francis M. Hayashi, Casper Y. Horikoshi, Kenneth T. Miyake, Frank Y. Ohtomo, Joseph Sakakibara, Harper Sakaue, Roy Sano, Roy Sasaki, Lester E. Suzuki, Alpha Takagi, Lloyd Wake, and Norio F. Yasaki. Southern California Arizona Conference received Peter Chen, Edward Iwamoto, T. J. Machida, Michael Morizono, James K. Sasaki, H. John Yamashita, and George Nishikawa. Edward Iwamoto was perhaps the youngest Nisei minister to enter the Pacific Japanese Provisional Annual Conference. Succeeding ministers would be Sansei or younger Japan-trained ministers and a few whites.

Oddly enough, the dissolution of the Japanese Conference came in the 1960s when the entire nation was in the struggle for civil rights and minority rights. The strong Japanese minority gave up its autonomy; they would enter another kind of struggle in the future years.

THE PERIOD OF THE SANSEI AND THE ASIAN CAUCUS

The postmerger period was a time when all the churches tried to adjust to their new Conference situations. Although they voted for the mergers, they really didn't belong in spirit in the new Conferences. Their psychology and activities were still ethnically oriented. The Japanese-speaking members could never fit into the new Conference life. The English-speaking ministers and lay people tried valiantly to work together with Japanese in Conference and district affairs, and some have done well, but in reality it was not a success. The Nisei women did the best job of participation, especially at district affairs and United Methodist Women and Church Women United.

Very soon after the merger, some isolated ministers became dissatisfied with their loneliness, so a movement for caucuses and all-Japanese gatherings was started. Having lost along with other Asians the power to influence appointments, the National Federation of Asian American United Methodists was organized in the mid-1970s. Jonah Chang was the first executive director, and he served for several years. Jonah Chang could speak Chinese, Japanese, English, and Mandarin. He served Japanese churches and founded Taiwanese church groups. When Chang left the Federation to become a superintendent, Naomi Southard succeeded him, one of a few Japanese American women ministers, along with Nancy Yamasaki (Bishop Wilbur Choy's wife). Under the Asian American Federation, the Advisory Committee on Asian American Ministries was started in 1970 to give suggestions to the Conference cabinets about appointments. It was purely advisory, so it had little if any power. Many unsatisfactory appointments were bound to be made because bishops and cabinets have little knowledge of Japanese and Asian churches. Under the Federation Asian caucuses worked to make the church at large understand the needs of Asian Methodists.

In this postmerger period the Sansei ministers take the limelight. In 1987 there were only two active Nisei ministers in the Western Jurisdiction serving primarily Japanese churches. The rest are Japan-trained ministers or white or Taiwanese ministers.

Asian youth camps have been successfully held; some of the leaders in this Asian camp movement are Grant Hagiya, Keith Inouye, Roger Morimoto, Mark Nakagawa, Mike Yoshii, and Robert Hoshibata. Others are involved in junior high and young adult camps through the Church Federation. Alpha Goto, Keith Sera, and seminarian Derek Nakano see some action here. Not too long ago the Nisei took the lead, but now it is almost entirely Sansei. Gary Oba is another Sansei gaining experience.

Among the Japanese churches Japanese-speaking ministers are in a minority, so they have a Japanese-speaking ministers' fellowship in which they can discuss their priorities. Frank Ohtomo, Jun Ehara, Toshikazu Kuwabara, Hidemi Ito, Jonathan Fujita, Harry Fujimoto, Hito Iwabuchi, and Izuru Aratani are part of this group. The last thirty years have seen a decline in ministry specifically targeted to Japanese, but there is renewed need for Japanese-speaking ministry for the thousands of new arrivals from Japan since the 1950s. How the Japanese Caucus treats Japanese-speaking ministry in the coming years is something that needs careful watching. And then there is the problem of how the Annual Conferences will treat Japanese-speaking ministers, because English is not one of their strong points.

Another avenue of growth open to Japanese and other Asians the last twenty-five years is service in the Methodist bureaucracy. Wilbur Choy, a Chinese American, and Roy Sano, a Japanese American, have been elected bishops. Several Japanese Americans have served or are serving as district superintendents, such as George Nishikawa, Michael Morizono, and Edward Iwamoto. A few have gone on to serve in the Board of Discipleship, such as Jiro Mizuno, Peter Chen, and Naomi Southard. Hidetoshi Tanaka is serving in the Commission on Religion and Race. Eleanor Kajiwara is a lay administrator in the Board of Discipleship. Lloyd Wake is serving well in the Glide Foundation Church.

However, it is the local church where the action is. Without the local churches there can be no larger church bodies. Success in the local church is the great test of ability. We need more leadership to make possible local church growth, as the Koreans are doing. The Nisei generation is fast going out of the picture, and the third generation and fourth generation, Sansei and Yonsei, are now taking the leadership, and we trust that they will recapture the faith and zeal and enthusiasm of the early founders of our Japanese Methodist churches, who started and built churches where there was not a thing to build on except people.

BIBLIOGRAPHY

Anonymous. *Life of Kanichi Miyama*. Manuscript in the author's personal library.

Campbell, Barbara. *United Methodist Women in the Middle of Tomorrow*. New York: Women's Division, General Board of Global Ministries, The United Methodist Church, 1983. Pamphlet.

Gospel Society Minutes, June 1881 to December 1897. Minutes of Fukuin Kai. Manuscript in the author's personal library.

Imaizumi, Genkichi. *Senkukyu Juken Miyama Kanichi To Sono Jidai* (Kanichi Miyama and his times). Nikon, Japan: Mikuni Press, 1940. Author's translation.

Journal of the California Conference of the Methodist Episcopal Church, 1877 to 1900.

Journal of the Pacific Japanese Methodist Episcopal Church Mission Conference, from 1901 to 1939.

Journal of the Pacific Japanese Provisional Annual Conference, 1940 to 1964.

Koga, Sumio, compiler. *A Centennial Legacy: History of the Japanese Christian Mission in North America, 1877–1977.* Vol. 1. Chicago: Norbart, 1977.

100th Anniversary History of Hakodate Church. Hokkaido, Japan: Hakodate Church, 1974. Booklet.

C H A P T E R 7

MOVEMENT OF SELF-EMPOWERMENT:

History of the National Federation of Asian American United Methodists

Jonah Chang

ETHNIC CAUCUS MOVEMENT

The caucus movement is primarily to affirm the identity of a people. For many yellow and brown[1] Christians, conversion to Christianity at one time meant the adoption of a "superior" form of Euro-American Christian art, music, architecture, and theology. Now through the movement we can celebrate the richness and joy of yellow and brown Christian faith.

The caucus movement is also a movement of self-empowerment. Through the movement, yellow and brown Christians hoped to have greater possibilities of becoming visible for their leadership ability, theological groundedness, and missional commitment.

Lastly, the caucus movement enables a people to "get its act together." Yellow and brown American Christians have learned that strategy can be economical, efficient, satisfying, biblical, and even amusing.

The National Federation of Asian American United Methodists (NFAAUM) has, in the last quarter of the twentieth century, missional tasks and roles to fulfill. It is like a sharp sword, valued for its cutting edge that strives to cut a shape and place for a viable Christian Church.

Shape, or more properly, the structure of the church, is our concern as a caucus. As stated in the Acts of the Apostles, new people were added daily to the church in Jerusalem. In chapter 6:1-6, the first ethnic caucus is credited with influencing the entire church. The twelve powerful Hebrew leaders looked at the ideas about which the Hellenists were "murmuring" (RSV), or "quarreling" (GNB) and worked out a solution that would be beneficial to everyone. As a result, a new structure was adopted to meet the needs of the growing church. History has proven that this was the turning point of global Christian interaction. Although the Hellenists were the minority in Jerusalem, they were the only group that had real potential for growth. Because their culture was widespread and linked to others beyond the sea, they helped to open other ethnic and cultural regions to the *evangelion*. Today, the twentieth-century parallel of the first-century Mediterranean world is the Pacific Rim, which is twenty or even thirty times greater in size than the Hellenistic world.

Ultimately, the Hellenistic caucus was more effective than the Jewish Christians in dealing with issues of organization. It provided the blueprint the church needed. It is vital for today's church to receive the talents of colorful Christians, the new Hellenists, in order that it may be reshaped.

Content is the other concern we bring to the church as a caucus. The past decade has seen a steady decline in membership among the mainline denominations. The caucus believes that the decline is because there is no spark to set the church aflame. It is not an overstatement to say that no one knows how to light the fire. Therefore, the most cherished self-professed role of the Asian American Christian caucus is to try to light the fire by means of *advocacy*. The biblical precedent for this is found in the word *parakletos* (John 14:26 [KJV], "Comforter, which is the Holy Ghost;" in I John 2:1 [RSV] we read "we have an advocate with the Father, Jesus Christ the righteous"). The NFAAUM as a caucus advocates for certain issues and in so doing focuses on the vision and/or motive aspects of actions taken to address issues. Another important element in *parakletos* is the life of the community of faith. The Johannine focus of *parakletos* is an emphasis on the life of the Christian community. The advocate-counselor becomes the key in liberating a sinful soul from its flesh and in empowering a weak faith to move toward a life of fulfillment. The advocate-counselor also acts to disturb the conscience of the oppressor and to convict the world of its sins.

The North American church today lacks vigor because many members want to hear tranquilizing words—comfortable and pleasing, but not disturbing. The church has not moved forward because it did not want the "fire" to burn—the fire ignited by the disturbing and colorful experiences and visions of its ethnic minorities. This was not so in the first generation of the Christian church. There were many fiery movements, and those who were touched, and those who heard, as described in Acts 2:37, "were pricked in their heart" (KJV).

The NFAAUM fosters identity, self-worth, and strength in this "alien land." At the same time, it keeps itself open to the power and inspiration of the gospel, which calls people to the ongoing task of mission and witness in the *oikoumene* ("household") of God.

HALT OF MISSIONAL CONCERN WITH INTEGRATION

The missional task of the Christian church was once dealt with by the "hinterland" approach. Those who were "learned," "gifted," and "blessed" tried to show compassion for the people who were "heathens," "uninformed," and "uncivilized," but they were also condescending. Mission was, and in the minds of many still is, to leave one's homeland, to lower one's standards of living and intelligence in order to lead a crusade and undertake the noble task of teaching religion. The goal was to raise the heathen people's "standard." Good Christians were taught Euro-American ways of music, worship, arts, and even language; there was no room for indigenized hermeneutics and theology, at least while the "hinterland" syndrome was alive and well. Sadly, the mission board knew only how to play on emotions, such as displaying pictures of hungry children. When people of color who do not share in the Euro-American ideology or cultural tradition begin to excel in science and technology, resentment of these "Christian" attitudes mounts and enthusiasm for mission diminishes. The blessed and chosen of God are supposedly the achievers and givers; the receivers, on the other hand, are over yonder in the hinterland.

Home mission has traditionally been observed as an afterthought of foreign mission. The Chinatown Mission in San Francisco started only after a missionary to China, Dr. Otis Gibson, returned and could not go back. Chinatown and its Chinese residents attracted the attention of California politicians and the power brokers of business and labor. The church, under the auspices of mission, entered the picture late in the game and could only serve as "rescuers" of the victims and the weak, in their struggle to survive.

Asian Americans could not possibly integrate with whites in business, labor, and the economy; however, integration was possible in the church. The church opened an avenue for Asian Christians to be equal and to be ordained into the ranks of the ministry. It was exciting for Christians of color to be able to obtain full status as "civilized" Christians. But integration was always just a myth. The best people of color could achieve was the "honorary white" status.

Still, Christians of color believed in the church's pronouncement of open itinerancy, opportunity of leadership, achievement ladders of salary and position, and higher pension benefits, among other things. As we look back in the 1950s and 1960s, it is apparent that the movements to disband the former Provisional Conferences were not based on the missional motif. The momentum of mission to Asian Americans was completely lost. The Oriental Provisional Conference, which consisted of Chinese, Filipino, and Korean churches, disbanded itself in 1956. The Pacific Japanese Provisional Conference disbanded itself and merged with regular Annual Conferences in 1964.

MISSIONAL REASONS FOR THE ASIAN AMERICAN
CAUCUS MOVEMENT

The results of mergers of Provisional Conferences with regular Conferences were so devastating that there was no single new church organized, no single new minister recruited, no single gathering of clergy and laity for fellowship or encouragement held. There was a total absence of plan or goal for ministry. The morale of Asian American ministers and lay people was very low, their sense of isolation pervasive.

In November 1967, four years after the last annual session of the Pacific Japanese Provisional Conference was held, Paul Hagiya and Jonathan Fujita, then pastors of Simpson Methodist Church in Denver, invited all pastors and laypeople of the former Japanese Provisional Conference to share in the dedication service of the newly constructed Simpson church building. Special efforts were made to invite the "delegates" to stay after the dedication to discuss the status of Japanese American ministries. The body that met, called the Pacific Methodist Fellowship (PMF), accepted the task of informing the general church of the growing concern over the fragmentation of Japanese American ministries as well as the need for a coordinated national strategy for this ministry. The bishop of the Denver area at the time, R. Marvin Stuart, heard the discussion and promised to carry the PMF's concerns to the Council of Bishops that convened on November 9–12 in Miami, Florida.

The issues of Japanese ministry were referred by the Council of Bishops to the National Division of the Board of Missions. Almost a year later the historical step toward the caucus movement took place in the form of three hearings in Los Angeles, San Francisco, and Seattle. Dr. Harry Komuro, executive secretary of National Division and former superintendent of the Hawaii Mission, spent October 1968 conducting the hearings. The Reverend Peter Chen, chair of the Pacific Japanese Fellowship and pastor of North Gardena United Methodist Church at that time, presided over the hearing. By the end of the hearings several acute needs emerged: (1) the need to undergird Asian American ministries with a theological base, (2) the need for freedom of interconference appointments, and (3) the need for a closer relationship with indigenous churches in Asia. Based on the three stated needs, Japanese United Methodists organized the Advisory Committee on Japanese Work, under the sponsorship of the National Division of the Board of Mission.

On February 3–4, 1969, the National Consultation of Japanese Work was called to gather at Pine United Methodist Church in San Francisco. An executive committee that took the form of consultants to the College of Bishops of the Western Jurisdiction was organized. The college assigned Bishop Charles Golden as the episcopal representative on that committee. The executive committee then recommended that a staff member be employed and that the committee be authorized to act as a personnel committee to the staff. The committee also projected a budget of $25,000 and submitted it to the National Division. A structure not spelled out in the *Book of Discipline,* which set the direction for the eventual formation of the Asian Caucus, began to take shape.

While the consultation on Japanese work was giving birth to its executive committee, it was also gathering the loose ends of ministries, or rather, missed ministries. A follow-up team was given responsibility to find ways to solve the concerns raised, such as facilitation of interconference appointments, issues regarding identity, and planning and implementation of programs in areas not adequately covered by Annual Conference structures. The possibility of staffing on a jurisdictional level was explored. Suggested responsibilities of this staff person included strengthening of Conference and jurisdictional ethnic ministries committees and of relationships between the different Asian subgroups within the Western Jurisdiction.

Having made detailed plans for the future, Asian American ministries needed to wait a few months, specifically until April 29, to transform these plans into reality. At the Executive Committee meeting of the National Division in New York on April 29, 1969, the following resolution was adopted, with a few added stipulations:

> That the National Division (in consultation with the College of Bishops and the several Boards of Mission of the Western Jurisdiction) authorize an Advisory Committee on Ethnic Language Ministries, to be advisory to and attached to the Service Unit of the Special Ministries of the Section of Home Fields. That the work be provided with adequate budget for one staff member. The Service Unit of Special Ministries shall explore and implement as far as practicable the recommendations of the Consultation on Japanese Work. It shall also work with other ethnic language minority groups.[2]

The National Division, in approving the resolution, included in the stipulations that the cooperation of the Western Jurisdiction would be actively sought, and that the recommendation would embrace not only Japanese work but also that of other Asian subgroups. The Finance Committee further stipulated that the National Division provide up to 50 percent of the "adequate budget for one staff member" ("adequate budget" meaning a figure between $20,000 and $25,000 per annum).

The recommendation on hiring staff for Asian American ministries, though late, would have kept Asian Americans on the agenda of United Methodists in mission. Unfortunately, staffing by the United Methodist mission arm was never implemented. Regretfully, The United Methodist Church, as symbolized in its Board of Missions, did not have any vision beyond *integration*. It took several decades of caucus movements following integration to recover the church's vision. The attempt to recapture the spirit has been only partially effective, considering the tremendous efforts expended to inspire, sensitize, and educate the whole church.

The suggestion of placing a staffperson from the Asian American community on the Board of Missions was not implemented. The following are the major reasons for this: (1) The Western Jurisdiction was never structured for program or personnel; (2) no Asian American was available on a national or jurisdictional level to hold the parties accountable to deliver on the pronouncements uttered; (3) unfortunately, the commitment of the Board of Missions was only 50 percent of the budget needed. This is a reflection of a half-hearted will for mission and ministry. History has proven that at a most crucial point, The United Methodist Church did not respond to its missional tasks.

The new immigration law proposed by President John F. Kennedy and signed by President Lyndon B. Johnson in 1965 started to take effect around 1969 to 1974. Immigration from Asian countries was increasing by leaps and bounds. Since then, for instance, new Chinese congregations using the methods of house churches and Bible study groups have mushroomed in California, especially in the metropolitan San Francisco and Los Angeles areas. However, United Methodists did not organize a single new church during the same period!

In order to implement the decision made in April 1969, the National Division invited fifty ministers from the churches of the two former Provisional Conferences and the College of Bishops of the Western Jurisdiction to discuss and plan for the future of Asian American ministries. At this meeting, held on March 11–12, 1970, a list of requests worked out by the churches and ministers was presented to the College of Bishops. Item number one on the request list specified that the executive committee of the Advisory Committee on Asian American Ministries be authorized to act as consultants on appointments to Asian American churches across Conference boundaries. Concurrent with the request for cross-Conference appointments was the request to affirm an open-pulpit covenant for Asian American ministers. Also on the request list was the consideration that the work of Asian American churches and ministers be on the College of Bishops' agenda at least once a year. Other requests included affirmation of ethnic ministries as a specialized ministry requiring specific orientation and particular training and skills; recognition of the seniority of ethnic ministers, particularly when a merger takes place between an ethnic and a white church; and that serious efforts be made to provide subsidies to raise the minimum salary of Asian American pastors to the average salary level of ministers in the Annual Conference.

The following year saw the beginning of a bona fide Asian American caucus. This beginning was not so much a matter of choice but the only possible alternative to recovering the loss of missional energy. Black Methodists for Church Renewal was organized while Asian Americans were groping for a missional structure. The Commission on Religion and Race, created at the 1968 General Conference, was considered to be the best agency to work on ethnic minority concerns of The United Methodist Church. A proposal submitted on January 26, 1971, seeking financial support for the staff and office of Research and Development of Asian American Ministries was approved at the Commission's Tampa, Florida, meeting on February 22 in the amount of $23,500. The 50 percent amount of support received from the National Division was not sufficient to implement the new structure. This fifty-fifty support, however, enabled the new organization to engage in something between mission and advocacy, which while full of imagination lacked a most important capacity to develop programs. The Asian American caucus decided to use the funds received from the National Division for the costs of research, planning, advice, and consultations.

A month later, the convocation on Asian American Ministries was held from March 11–14, 1971, at the Surfrider Inn in Santa Monica, California. The following resolution adopted at the convocation served to mark the inauguration of the Asian American caucus:

> We the Asian American Caucus of the United Methodist Church, which includes at the present time, Chinese, Filipino, Japanese, Korean, and any other groups who have similar ethnic roots, acknowledge the heritage that is peculiarly ours as Asians who have been a part of the United Methodist Church. While acknowledging the values of this heritage, we recognize that our participation within the United Methodist Church has been only partial and limited, and that our identity as Asians has been in terms of Euro-American values and culture. We affirm that the Asian American Caucus is at present the most viable means to achieve:
>
> 1. Self-determination to develop relevant Christian Mission strategies on the local, annual conference, and national levels.
> 2. Openness to explore and to appreciate the values of our ethnic cultural and religious heritages that make the gospel relevant and meaningful to Asian Americans.
> 3. Liberation from the elements of racism within the United Methodist Church and society.
> We recognize the need to understand and to cooperate with other ethnic caucus groups within the United Methodist Church.[3]

The convocation was attended by pastors and laypersons from practically all of the then-existing thirty-eight churches in the Western Jurisdiction. All five bishops in the jurisdiction were present and participated in the group discussions, exploring new ways to advance Asian American ministries. Dr. Woodie W. White of the Commission on Religion and Race was the keynote speaker at the banquet on Saturday night, March 13.

The participants, recognizing the importance of being a consultative body, decided to constitute themselves as a caucus to implement the move toward self-determination and self-identity within The United Methodist Church. It approved the existing Advisory Committee on Asian American Ministries as constituted at the March 1970 meeting of fifty ministers. Peter Chen chaired the committee, made up of the Reverend Lester Suzuki (Japanese), the

Reverend Wilbur W. Y. Choy (Chinese), and Bishop Charles Golden (Council of Bishops).

The convocation preceded the election of delegates to General and Jurisdictional Conference, so the process of electing an Asian American bishop in the forthcoming 1972 Jurisdictional Conference began at the convocation.

Following the convocation, the advisory committee, acting as the search committee for the newly created office of Research and Development of Asian American Ministries, selected the Reverend George Nishikawa to be the executive director. The work began on July 1, 1971, at Lake Park United Methodist Church in Oakland, California.

The following year the second convocation of Asian American United Methodists of the Western Jurisdiction was held in Seattle, Washington, in the month of July, to precede the Jurisdictional Conference. The convocation adopted the recommendation that the distribution of participating delegates from the Annual Conferences to the Asian American Advisory Committee be fairly even. It also reconfirmed the relationship between the National Division and the Advisory Committee; Dr. Harry Komuro represented the National Division in negotiating the goals and strategies of Asian American ministry. A decision was made to assign the advisory committee a dual role—that of coordinating committee to Asian American communities in the jurisdiction and that of advisory committee to the National Division of the Board of Missions. Also, nominations of Asian Americans to the general boards and agencies for at-large election were made for the first time; nominees were selected by a written ballot in which participants named qualified candidates. The Reverend Lloyd Wake, the first Asian American episcopal candidate, was named, and the convocation worked on strategy and support for his election. The following week Wilbur W. Y. Choy, however, was elected as the first Asian American bishop by the Jurisdictional Conference.

In 1973 George Nishikawa was appointed to the superintendency of the Los Angeles District of the Southern California-Arizona Conference. The petition of executive director was open for a new search. Jonah Chang was selected to begin his term from July 1, 1973, and the name of the office was changed to Asian American Ministries of the Western Jurisdiction.

FORMATION OF THE NATIONAL CAUCUS

The third convocation of Asian American United Methodists of the Western Jurisdiction was held October 10–12, 1974, at Leamington Hotel in Oakland, California. This event marked the beginning of the NFAAUM. Unlike its predecessors, the convocation was open to Asian American leaders from outside the Western Jurisdiction. Among the participants from other jurisdictions were Dr. Wonmo Dong, Espie del Rosario, Victor Fujiu,

Chan-Hie Kim, Abraham New, Amos Rhee, the Reverend Perry Saito, Myong-Gul Son, and the Reverend Dr. Peter Sun. It was not surprising that the convocation decided to expand its scope to form a national caucus of Asian American United Methodists. A seven-member task force was directed by the convocation to convene in Dallas in February 1975, immediately after the Interethnic Consultation sponsored by the Commission on Religion and Race in San Antonio, Texas.

Members of the Task Force were the Reverend Stanley De Pano, Wonmo Dong, the Reverend Masaji Goto, the Reverend David Harada, the Reverend Dr. Chan-Hie Kim, the Reverend Abraham New, Perry Saito, the Reverend Dr. Roy Sano, Peter Sun, Mrs. Sue Yee, and Jonah Chang (staff). The Task Force drafted the bylaws and proposed that the name of the new organization be the National Federation of Asian American United Methodists and that the office of Asian American Ministries of the Western Jurisdiction be made the national office. The Task Force also asked the Asian American Ministries office to prepare for the first annual meeting to be held on April 11–12, 1975, at Essex Inn in Chicago.

Wonmo Dong, chair of the task force, convened the first annual board of directors' meeting. Those invited to witness the beginning of the NFAAUM and participate in decision making were ten delegates from the Western Jurisdiction and four each from the remaining four jurisdictions, totaling twenty-six members. At the opening celebration, Bishop Choy expressed the following sentiments:

> We are here gathered . . . for the establishing of the National Federation of Asian American United Methodists. We have announced these as our objectives (Article II of Bylaws) (a) to form a national federation of the United Methodist Church; (b) to articulate the concerns, interests and needs of the Asian American constituencies in all Jurisdictions of the Church; (c) to advocate the causes of Asian Americans before appropriate boards and agencies of the Church; (d) to coordinate the activities of the Jurisdictional Asian American Caucuses in relationship with boards and agencies of the General Church; (e) to promote relevant and meaningful Asian American ministries at all levels of the Church; and (f) to encourage full participation of Asian American United Methodists in all aspects of the life of the Church.[4]

At the time of chartering the National Federation, the basic assumption of the organization was that Asian American United Methodists should participate through the jurisdictional grouping. However, at the time of formation of the NFAAUM, there were only two organized Asian American caucuses, Northeastern and Western. Actually there were very few Asian American local churches in the North Central, South Central, and Southeastern Jurisdictions.

While all jurisdictions were organizing to form Asian American caucuses, new movement among subethnic groups was also taking place. Major subethnic caucuses were organized. Among the Chinese, Filipino, Japanese, and Korean caucuses, the Korean caucus became more and more visible due to the pressure of Korean churches in all five jurisdictions. Among many resolutions adopted by the first National Federation board was the Korean proposal to hold a Korean United Methodist Convocation with clergy and lay persons scheduled for June 19–21, 1975, in Denver, Colorado. In the resolution it was estimated that there were about 110 Korean Methodist clergy spread throughout the United States. Within two years after the formation of the National Federation, the national ethnic caucuses demanded linkage with the NFAAUM. As a result, the bylaws of the NFAAUM–1977 were changed to accommodate as members of the Board two persons from each of the five Jurisdictions and one person from each of the four ethnic caucuses. Seven at-large slots were added to create balance between lay and clergy representatives and to include women, young adults, and other Asian American groups. The total number of persons on the board was twenty-one.

In 1978 the Filipinos and Formosans were recognized as ethnic caucuses; in 1979 the Asian American women's group was accepted as a special interest group; and in 1981 the South Asian National Caucus was accepted as the newest ethnic group of the NFAAUM. Each caucus mentioned obtained one seat on the board of directors on the year of its recognition. So by the year 1983 there were twelve tribes—five jurisdictional, six ethnic, and one women's group—in the NFAAUM family.

TEN YEARS OF NATIONAL FEDERATION ACTIVITY

In 1975 the board of directors decided to move the office of executive director from Oakland-Lake Park United Methodist Church to San Francisco-Glide United Methodist Church.

Only a few weeks earlier, the General Council on Ministries (GCOM) in March 1975 created a task force of twenty-nine persons headed by the late Reverend George Outen to hold consultations on the ethnic minority local church in United Methodism. The Asian American consultation was held in Oakland, California. The findings of the four ethnic consultations were reported to the GCOM in December 1975. The 1975 NFAAUM board of directors decided to immediately join the interethnic coalition for addressing the crisis of the ethnic minority churches and leadership. A document prepared by the task force and adopted by the GCOM was presented to the 1976 General Conference in Portland, Oregon.

The second annual board of directors' meeting of the NFAAUM was held on March 26–27, 1976, at Simpson United Methodist Church in Denver, Colorado. The NFAAUM board spent considerable time in distributing the

$45,000 grant received from the National Division of the General Board of Global Ministries. Grants were made to jurisdictional and ethnic caucuses, ranging from $720 to $4,741.50. Among other items of business, the Task Force on Human Rights and Social Justice in Asia was organized. The board of directors also voted to support ethnic minority congregation and leadership development as the missional priority of The United Methodist Church at the 1976 General Conference. However, at the General Conference a triad-priority was adopted. By so doing The United Methodist Church created a situation in which the ethnic minority congregations priority competed with the emphases on world hunger and evangelism.

Before the Denver annual board of directors' meeting, the delegates of the NFAAUM met in early March in St. Louis with the Asian Pacific Section of the World Division of the General Board of Global Ministries. The purpose was to establish a new program of mission partnership with Asian colleague churches. A task force with members from both the NFAAUM and the World Division was organized to recommend specific models of mission exchange to be implemented from 1977. The NFAAUM also advocated strongly for an Asian American staff position in the Language and Ethnic Ministries Department in the National Division of the General Board of Global Ministries. The result was that Dr. Myong-Gul Son, member of the North Texas Annual Conference, was appointed to begin his work in the summer of 1976.

During the two years following the initiation of the National Asian Caucus, the growth of the Korean constituency was phenomenal. The request by the Koreans at the 1975 NFAAUM annual board meeting for special resources was met, and in 1976 a self-assessment and national strategy meeting was held. The national Korean caucus was named the Association of Korean American United Methodist Churches. By the time of the 1977 NFAAUM board meeting, it was estimated that the Korean caucus was as large as, if not greater than, the Japanese caucus.

The third annual board of directors' meeting of the NFAAUM was held March 25–26, 1977, in Los Angeles. The board intentionally related to Asian American local churches by visiting Asian American churches and communities in the greater Los Angeles area. Representatives of the General Program Boards were present to express their concerns for Asian American ministries. Dr. Melvin Talbert, General Secretary of the Board of Discipleship, was an especially valuable resource to this annual meeting. At this meeting, Dr. Anatalio Ubalde was elected to be the second chairperson of the NFAAUM.

From March 31 to April 1, 1978, the fourth annual board of directors' meeting was held in Newark, New Jersey. Asian American churches, particularly Korean, had grown noticeably in the Northeastern Jurisdiction. Their leaders included Michael Hahm, Justin Haruyama, Hae Jong Kim, Moses Lee, Myong-Gul Son, Peter Sun, and Samuel Wong. Through this annual meeting the National Federation intended to establish stronger ties with Asian American churches in the Eastern Seaboard and also to become acquainted with the staff of the Board of Global Ministries, Commission of Christian Unity and Inter-religious Concerns, Board of Church and Society, and the Commission on Religion and Race. The need to gather Asian American United Methodist people for affirmation, fellowship, learning, and empowerment was strongly advocated at this meeting.

The first National Convocation of Asian American Churches was held December 6 to 12, 1978, in San Francisco. Nearly five hundred Asian Americans assembled from all across the country. Present at this historic gathering were Bishop Wilbur W. Y. Choy, general secretaries, staff members of general boards and agencies, and most of the Asian American pastors and lay representatives from almost all Asian American churches. Bishop Choy, Pastor Wake, and Dr. Sano were among the major speakers and leaders of the convocation. It was the first gathering of such magnitude ever to be held among all the Protestant denominations. The event was significantly marked by Asian Americans' search for unity despite diversity of background. One of the most important resolutions adopted was to work together with other ethnic minority caucuses to present the ethnic minority local church missional priority for the 1981–1984 quadrennium.

The fifth annual board of directors' meeting of the NFAAUM was held on March 30–31, 1979, in San Francisco. Peter Sun of Washington, D.C., was elected as the chairperson. Melvin Talbert was invited to speak on why and how to achieve interethnic accord. Also, under his leadership the strategy and data gathering leading toward the presentation of the missional priority "Developing and Strengthening the Ethnic Minority Local Church" to the General Conference was underway. In partnership with the NFAAUM and the National Division of the Board of Global Ministries, Asian Americans went a step further to envision more concrete goals and strategies for the missional priority. The result was articulated in a brochure *Ripe For Harvest,* which was the Asian American supplement to the 1980 Missional Priority operational manual. It was recommended to the NFAAUM annual meeting (1980) and was referred to all subcaucuses and general program boards for implementation.

The sixth annual board of directors' meeting of the NFAAUM was held on April 12–14 in Indianapolis, Indiana, immediately preceding the 1980 General Conference. The recommendation to create a coordinating committee on Asian American ministries, contained in the *Ripe For Harvest* document, was discussed at length. Because of strong opposition from Asian American staff members and their suggestion to seriously consider the quadrennial report of the Commission on Religion and Race, and NFAAUM board of directors killed the petition, which would have enabled Asian Americans to participate in the program coordination of the missional priority. Instead, it was recommended that the Asian American Ministries Task Force be lodged under the Commission on Religion and Race (a monitoring agency). Although the recommendation would not provide significant help to Asian American ministry, it was historic in that the General Conference recognized the role of the NFAAUM by mandating "the Commission on Religion and Race in consultation with the National Federation of Asian American United Methodists, appoint a Task Force on Asian American ministries to study, recommend, coordinate, and monitor the development of ministries among Asian Americans in the nation."[5]

In Indianapolis Asian American United Methodists were among the diligent forces that forged the strategies toward the approval of developing and strengthening the ethnic minority local church as the sole missional priority of The United Methodist Church.

For the Jurisdictional Conferences of 1980, the NFAAUM supported Hae Jong Kim of Northeastern, Perry Saito of North Central, and Roy Sano of Western as candidates for the episcopacy. There was no election of an Asian American that year.

From November 13–15, 1980, all new Asian American general boards and agencies' directors and staff members were invited to meet in San Francisco with the National Federation leaders. The main purposes were (1) to learn the holistic view of the denomination, the status of Asian American churches, and how to work with boards and agencies for the enhancement of Asian American ministries and (2) to formulate an Asian American comprehensive plan for the new quadrennium.

In 1981 the U.S. census of 1980 was published. The Asian population had increased by 128 percent from the 1970 figure. According to the report, there were 806,027 Chinese, 774,640 Filipinos, 700,747 Japanese, and 354,529 Koreans. For many decades up to this point, Japanese Americans were considered to be the largest group. Asian American United Methodists increased in general. However, the growth of Korean churches was phenomenal. In fifteen years from 1965, the number of Korean churches grew from 6 to about 120—a 2,000 percent increase!

The seventh annual meeting of the board of directors of the NFAAUM was held on March 27–29, 1981, in Los Angeles. The Reverend Leo Hsu, pastor of the Chinese United Methodist Church in Los Angeles, was elected as the fourth chair of the NFAAUM. The work of collecting Asian and Asian American hymns was in progress, so the occasion was utilized to introduce some of these hymns to non-Asian communities. A dinner and hymn festival held on March 4 at Wilshire United Methodist Church attracted nearly a thousand people. I-to Loh designed and directed the festival, and church leaders organized the dinner and presentation of choirs. The festival was repeated on October 10 in Palo Alto, California.

The work of compiling *Hymns from the Four Winds* was completed in January 1982. However, it was not until 1983 that Abingdon Press was able to publish the hymnal—in time for the second Convocation of Asian American United Methodist Churches in April.

The eighth annual board of directors' meeting of the NFAAUM was held on April 22–25, 1982, at Perkins School of Theology in Dallas. A Planning Committee was organized for the second convocation. Peter Sun was asked to chair the planning committee, and the 4-H Center of Chevy Chase, Maryland, was picked as the site.

During the year 1982, July 28 to August 1, the first National Ecumenical Convocation of Pacific and Asian American Churches was held in Berkeley, California. Since United Methodist resources were reserved for the 1983 convocation, only the Western Jurisdiction participated in this historic ecumenical convocation.

The second National Convocation of Asian American United Methodist Churches was held April 6–10, 1983. About four hundred persons from around the country gathered for inspiration, mission studies, and workshops on strategies for leadership and empowerment. One significant event was the decision to kick off the Asian American endowment with the goal of raising $5 million. The decision to initiate the endowment fund was coupled with the organization of its central leadership team, chaired by Peter Chen of San Jose, California.

The convocation also threw its unanimous support behind Hae Jong Kim, Perry Saito, and Roy Sano in their candidacy for the episcopacy. Politically, it was important that as many Asian Americans as possible be elected to General Conference, and all three candidates needed to be among the delegations. A few months later, sixteen Asian Americans were elected to the 1984 General Conference. This number was an all-time high for Asian Americans, but it represented only 1.7 percent of the United Methodist delegates from the United States. Asian American episcopal candidates Perry Saito and Roy Sano were among those elected, and Hae Jong Kim was elected as first alternate from his Annual Conference. In addition to the General Conference delegates, twelve delegates were elected to the Jurisdictional Conferences of 1984.

The ninth NFAAUM annual board of directors' meeting was held on April 4–5, 1983, at the site of the second national convocation. Lloyd Wake was elected to chair the Federation for the second time. The ninth annual meeting will be remembered for its drastic overhaul of the bylaws of the NFAAUM. The proposed change was to give one seat each on the board to jurisdictional, ethnic, and special interest caucuses. The remainder of the slots on the board would be filled by the quadrennial gathering of the General Assembly. The subsequent ratification of the new by-laws by the jurisdictional caucuses was completed before the tenth annual meeting, held in 1984. This allowed the tenth annual meeting to set the date and the purpose of the first General Assembly, scheduled for 1985.

The tenth NFAAUM annual board of directors' meeting was held on April 28–29, 1984 at Harbor City Inn, Baltimore, Maryland, immediately preceding the 1984 General Conference. The caucus annual meeting was primarily a strategy session in which all General Conference delegates and twenty-five Asian American communicators conferred on how to support issues and petitions pertinent to Asian American ministries. The NFAAUM strongly supported "Developing and Strengthening the Ethnic Minority Local Church: For Witness and Mission" as the missional priority, instead of "Church Alive," proposed by the General Council on Ministries. The petition from the National Association of Korean American United Methodist Churches to create a language missionary conference was also endorsed by the caucus. Other Asian American petitions included "Doubling of UM Membership in two quadrennia," "Tithing be minimum norm of UM giving," and "Nuclear-Free Pacific."

The Inter-ethnic Strategy Group, a coalition of Asian, black, Hispanic, and Native American caucuses, had organized its constituents and supporters around the issue of the missional priority. The twenty-five Asian American communicators did on-site research, coordination, and facilitation of intra- and interracial strategies. All ethnic minority people were elated when the Inter-ethnic Strategy Group proposal was adopted over the powerful "majority" proposal submitted by the General Council on Ministries. Thus "Developing and Strengthening of the Ethnic Minority Local Church: For Witness and Mission" was made the missional priority of the quadrennium 1985–1988. The theology and operational guide written by the Inter-ethnic Group, edited by Roy Sano, became the official manual of the priority. The NFAAUM again was given the power to provide input into the "structure" of the church through its two voting members on the Missional Priority Coordinating Committee.

The 1984 General Conference also approved the organization of a "Missional Structure" instead of a language missionary conference for the Koreans. Immediate authorization was given to the National Division of the Board of Global Ministries and the Council of Bishops to work out a plan to enhance the mission of Koreans in the United States.

On July 18, 1984, during the session of Western Jurisdictional Conference in Boise, Idaho, the Reverend Dr. Roy I. Sano was elected bishop of The United Methodist Church and assigned to the Denver area. He is the second Asian American elected to the highest position of the church. Since two other candidates were not elected and since Bishop Choy had retired during the same session, Bishop Sano became the only Asian American bishop on active duty. The new bishop, the first Japanese American one, was on hand to head the celebration of the centennial year of the first appointment of a Japanese minister, Kanichi Miyama, in the Methodist church in the United States, held in October 1984 at Pine United Methodist Church in San Francisco.

The year 1985 marked the tenth anniversary of the NFAAUM. The celebration was held in conjunction with its first General Assembly on January 31–February 2, 1985, at the Meridien Hotel in San Francisco. The number of General Assembly delegates exceeded 175—a first for Asian American local churches. Never before had so many Asian American local churches taken full financial responsibility for sending so many delegates to a national gathering. The emphasis of the General Assembly was for the general program boards and national leaders to listen to the local church. Delegates were in the position of giving direction to boards and agencies, unlike past convocations where delegates gathered for study and listened to reports from national leaders and agencies. "So as Asian hymns were sung and prayers were offered in Asian languages at the opening worship, one could not help but feel that after ten years of caucus ministry, leadership has finally truly reached the grassroots level."[6]

With the General Assembly, the new structure of the National Federation took effect. Of the twenty-seven board members, fourteen were selected by their respective subcaucuses; the remaining thirteen at-large members were elected from the floor of the assembly. Tension mounted during the report of the nominations committee, which indicated that of the thirteen nominees, five were Korean and only one was Filipino. Filipino delegates voiced strong objection to this report. Several parliamentary procedures were attempted to have the committee or the plenary session revise the report, but each failed. Consequently, they staged a walkout of the assembly. Although Filipinos are the largest segment of the Asian American population, they felt that they were a powerless minority not only in The United Methodist Church but also in the NFAAUM. The caucus felt that this issue needed to be addressed early in the upcoming meetings.

The subsequent board of directors' meeting produced a new and historic chairperson, the Reverend Sivaji Subramaniam of Dayton, Ohio, the first South Asian to head the NFAAUM.

During the General Assembly, a farewell party was held to honor Jonah Chang, who had served as the first and only executive director of the National Federation for the past ten years. He resigned when appointed to be the district superintendent of the Bayview District in the California-Nevada Annual Conference.

As a result of the April 15–16, 1985, executive committee meeting and the subsequent mail-in ballot of the board of directors of the NFAAUM, the Reverend Naomi Southard of San Francisco was elected to succeed Jonah

Chang. With vigor and vision she is leading the NFAAUM into its second decade.

LESSONS FROM HISTORY

The disbanding of the Provisional Annual Conferences and the integration of ethnic churches into the regular Annual Conference structure were steps in the right direction. The United Methodist Church should feel a sense of accomplishment and continue to make the diversity and colorfulness of the church a reality to celebrate. However, it was a sad chapter in history when the church deemed there was no further need to focus on Asian American ministries. The church in the 1950s and 1960s did not create a handle to assist Asian Americans and to ease their pain when morale was low. At the time of merger no one could foresee (1) the rapid growth of the Asian immigrant population and the increased potential for growth of the Asian American Christian community; (2) the inordinate value placed on larger churches because of their ability to provide ministerial support, pressuring smaller Asian American churches into a defensive position; or (3) that under the noble banner of "connectionalism," a survival instinct rather than a vision of mission would dictate a "protectionalism" stance by the church.

In 1952 the McCarran-Walter Act made it possible for Asians not born in the United States to become naturalized. Although the act set an immigration quota of one hundred per year for Asian countries, the entire atmosphere of the Asian American community changed; those who had been in the United States since the turn of the century were now able to make the United States their home country. Thousands of Asian Americans acquired U.S. citizenship in the memorable 1950s, when the country was recovering from World War II. Then in 1965 the National Origins Act further changed the course of immigration in the United States. The act raised the Asian immigration quota to twenty thousand per year for Asian countries—the same as for European countries. The classification of aliens was changed to country of birth rather than race; this new realization of "justice and equality for all" resulted in massive numbers of Asian students-turned-professionals seeking permanent residence in the United States. Tens of thousands of Asians sought to remain and contribute their entire lives to their adopted country in the 1960s.

One of the most apparent results of this immigration is the growth of Chinese congregations in the San Francisco Bay Area between 1970 and 1985. In 1970 it was estimated that there were 15 Chinese Christian churches in the greater San Francisco Bay Area. Of the 15, 2 were United Methodist. In 1985 there were more than 150 congregations in the area, with only 4 being United Methodist churches.

Soon after the mergers, Asian American churches found that they were too widely scattered for effective and coordinated work. There was no longer a board of mission, education, or ordained ministry that could focus on their needs or the potentials of any particular language and ethnic group. There was no longer a holistic plan of recruitment, cultivation, and deployment of ministerial leadership. Because of language barriers and preoccupation with local church matters, ministers began insulating their local churches from connectional functions. It became a common practice of some ethnic congregations and retiring ministers to take the initiative in filling a vacancy by recruiting a successor from an Asian country who was very likely alien to United Methodist polity.

Although unable to fill all the needs of Asian American United Methodists, the caucus has been an effective alternative by which persons could participate in The United Methodist Church. To the Asian American, the caucus has always been missional and pastoral. Asian Americans know that being ad hoc, the caucus is temporary. But because of its voice of advocacy and concern, its lasting contributions will remain with the church. The action of the 1984 General Conference to adopt the minority report and make "Developing and Strengthening the Ethnic Minority Local Church: For Witness and Mission" the missional priority is a good example. The Inter-Ethnic Strategy Development Group proved it could stand up to a powerful body—the General Council on Ministries!

The present time can be likened to that following Pentecost, when people were amazed to see wondrous things in the followers of Christ—varieties of language spoken, diversities of backgrounds and traditions unified by mission. This is the era of ethnic minorities, and like the Christians in the book of Acts (2:12), their vision and commitment give birth to a silent explosion that ultimately leads to a new global destiny for humankind. When the disciples in Antioch were called Christians, they were being discriminated against; however, the disciples did not seem to be a bit worried (11:26). Christians were those who belonged to "the Way" (9:2); were concerned with refugees, widows, and orphans (6:1-2); were intoxicated with "new wine" (2:13); sought to listen to God rather than to men (4:19). They were the people who, led by the Spirit and the life and faith they experienced in Jerusalem for just a few decades, became historical and global in significance. Likewise, Asian Americans in today's world, through their connections with Asia and with a revitalized Christianity, are in a strategic position to change the course of world history.

NOTES

1. Usually Asian Americans are represented as yellow; however, there are many Asians who would rather be called brown, such as Indians, Filipinos, Indonesians, and Malaysians.

2. Minutes of the National Division Meeting, General Board of Global Ministries, Apr. 29, 1969.

3. Minutes of the American Ministries Convocation, Mar. 11–14, 1971. Available from the NFAAUM, 330 Ellis Street, San Francisco, CA.

4. Minutes of the Board of Directors Meeting of the NFAAUM, Apr. 11–13, 1975. Also available from the NFAAUM.

5. Anonymous, *Daily Christian Advocate,* 1980 General Conference.

6. Helen Chang, *AA News* 12, no. 9 (Feb. 1, 1985).

I N D E X